THE BRADY'S BEND FLOOD OF 1980

TRAGEDY IN WESTERN PENNSYLVANIA

LISA OLSZAK ZUMSTEIN

THE History PRESS

Published by The History Press
An imprint of Arcadia Publishing
Charleston, SC
www.historypress.com

First published 2025

Manufactured in the United States

ISBN 9781467170123

Library of Congress Control Number: 2025936192

Notice: The information in this book is true and complete to the best of our knowledge. It is offered without guarantee on the part of the author or The History Press. The author and The History Press disclaim all liability in connection with the use of this book.

DEDICATED TO THOSE WHO PERISHED

Information about those who perished was gathered from interviews with their family and friends. Each had a rich and full life and is profoundly missed by those who loved them. A list of survivors from 1980 is provided for each victim. Many of those individuals have since died.

Wilson "Butch" (39) and Betty Ellen Robinson (34) and Their Daughter, Amy (4)

As the youngest of six brothers, Butch Robinson knew the value of family. He lived alongside two of his brothers, their wives and his wife's parents. With their four homes side by side, the families loved gathering along the creek for a campfire, a game of horseshoes and some beer. Butch enjoyed snowmobiling with his brothers.

Shy and timid, Betty Ellen treasured spending time with her family and close friends. As a teen, she fell in love with Butch and left school her senior year to marry. She adored her children, Thomas "T-Turtle" and Amy. Always close to her mother's side, Amy was a happy and content child.

Butch and Betty Ellen were survived by their son, Thomas "T-Turtle," who was sixteen in 1980. Butch was survived by five brothers, Clifford, Stuart, Paul, Eugene and Homer, and one sister, Mrs. Jerry (Margaret) Foster.

Butch, Betty Ellen and Amy Robinson. *Barry Robinson.*

Betty Ellen was also survived by her parents, Thomas and Betty Lias; two brothers, Richard and Robert Shepherd; two sisters, Mrs. Phillip (Beatrice) Coast and Mrs. Wayne (Lois) Heister; and her grandmother Mrs. Mabel Shepherd.

Elrick "Elick" (69) and Bertha "Birch" Custer (61) and Jerry Potts Jr. (2)

After working for the railroad, Elick opened Custer's TV and Appliance store in East Brady. He was a mild-mannered man who was well known for his TV repair services. It was not unusual to see him entering a home with a large carrying case full of TV parts and picture tubes. Birch Custer was a small woman who adored her family. She mirrored the meticulous upkeep of her home with the serene charm of wild ferns and rhododendrons that encircled the porch overlooking the creek.

As caretakers for Jerry Jr. during his mother, Myrtle's, work week, Elick and Berch had a truly special relationship with their grandson. Myrtle was the only child of Elick and Birch. Her son, Jerry Potts Jr., was survived by

Elrick and Bertha Custer, Jerry Potts Jr., Myrtle and Jerry Potts Sr., and Tina (Custer) Sullivan. *Jeanne (Potts) Guy.*

Myrtle; his father, Jerry Potts; a stepsister, Jeanne (Potts) Guy; and Myrtle's first son, Michael Riding. Jeanne, who was eight in 1980, recalls looking forward to playing with her only sibling, her baby brother, Jerry Jr., during visits with her father and Myrtle. She also recalls how she and Jerry Jr. enjoyed popsicles on the Custer porch.

Betty Kaufman (42)

Betty was a mother to her daughter, Deborah "Debbie" and sons, Michael "Mike" and Rick. Her life revolved around her children and grandchildren. They knew she'd be there when they arrived home from school. Her children's visiting friends said she was like a second mother. Besides watching over them, she welcomed them into her home with warmth and food.

Sunday dinners were a family tradition, and Betty had a reputation for cooking outstanding lasagna. Her baked goods were unmatched. You name it, she made it. She also loved a clean house; her mop sat in a bucket, always ready. She enjoyed collecting Avon perfumes and colognes, as well as bowling and playing bingo.

Betty Kaufman and Deborah (Kaufman) Hertweck. *Glenda Kaufman.*

Betty was survived by her husband, Walter Kaufman; two sons, Rick and Michael (married to Glenda); a daughter, Mrs. Randy (Deborah) Hertweck; two grandchildren; her mother, Mrs. Stella Kiser; a brother, Harry Kiser; and three sisters, Mrs. Clyde (Mildred) Griffiths, Mrs. Archie (Alice) Groves and Mrs. Thomas (Doris) Bearfield.

Carol Ann Lege (22)

Intelligent and well-liked with a contagious smile, Carol was the youngest of three children. In 1980, her older brother Dan and his wife, Paulette, had two daughters (Melissa, seven, and Mandi, four). Carol adored her nieces, and they adored her. She was also survived by her sister Mrs. Donald (Michelle) Pasko and her parents, Martin and Clara Lege.

Petite, with light brown hair and brown eyes, Carol had many talents. When in high school, she wrote for the school paper as well as for the local newspaper. Her English teacher said she was one of the best writers she had ever taught. She excelled in math and was on the homecoming court and in the National Honor Society. After completing her teaching degree at Indiana University of Pennsylvania in 1979, she started as a business teacher at Union High School. At the end of her first year, she and her best friend and elementary school teacher, Patty (McConville) DeBiasio, chaperoned the senior trip.

Carol and Patty's friendship started when they were in ninth grade. They were roommates at Indiana University of Pennsylvania and worked as teachers together at Union School District. After Carol's death, as a part of her own healing process, Patty wrote a poem that she dedicated to Carol.

Pieces of a shattered smile
Roll gently down my cheek
To think that somehow years have passed
And answers I still seek.

Feeling buried deep within
Have surfaced to my brain
Searching for good memories
But somehow finding pain.

Confusion, desperation,
Abandonment, distrust,
Loneliness, guilt and sadness
I'll let them go—I must!

Pieces of a special smile
Roll gently down my cheek
To think that God is here right now
To help me when I'm weak.

Carol goofing off with her friend Patty Niece Melissa Lege. Carol can be seen in the center, holding her niece Mandi Lege. On the right is her mother, Clara Lege. *Patty (McConville) DeBiasio; Dan and Paulette Lege.*

Hester Lenora (Toni) Crissman (67)

Born in 1913, Toni (Markel) Crissman grew up in a large family with four sisters and three brothers. She and her husband, Pete, had two sons, Ronald P. "Paul" and Gilbert "Gip." Described as a woman with a lot of spice and the boss of her household, she wasn't afraid to stand her ground with her husband, sons or her sons' visiting friends. Although she was a small woman, she was daunting. She and her husband cultivated a backyard garden.

Toni was survived by her husband, Pete Crissman, and their son Ronald "Paul" Crissman. Their son Gilbert was deceased at the time of the flood.

No photos are available for Mrs. Crissman.

CONTENTS

PREFACE

What started as a casual evening with friends in the safety of a home, a refuge from a terrible storm, ended with the death of nine innocent people, two of whom were children.

Betty Ellen Robinson; her husband, Butch; and their four-year-old daughter, Amy, were at home. Betty Ellen and her friend Mary were hosting a home sales party. As the evening rain worsened and the flooding began, Butch decided they needed to move to higher ground. Whether they stayed in place or fled their home, fate was not on their side.

Homebound Toni Crissman was alone, recovering from a recent surgery and moving through her house with a walker. Her husband was in the hospital addressing his own health crisis. Did Toni hear the water roaring through the valley before it overtook her? No one knows.

Elick and Berch Custer were babysitting their two-year-old grandson, Jerry, in their idyllic home, nestled in a valley amid the sound of the creek's peaceful ripples. Their one-story aluminum-sided house with huge ferns and purple rhododendron enfolding the back porch was transformed by a monstrosity of water that tore through its foundation. A malicious form of nature washed them away, along with three visitors who were seeking shelter from the storm. One of the six escaped death by clinging to a tree. The five others were gone.

Nine dead. A community destroyed. A catastrophic rainstorm of the kind that the community had never seen before and hasn't since.

The community was a rural oasis: Brady's Bend, Pennsylvania. Closeknit families and friends, often one and the same, thrived among the difficulties and beauty of their interconnected lives.

On Thursday, August 14, 1980, they found that their familiar customs of celebration, struggle and triumph were about to be tested in unimaginable ways.

That night, ten of the eleven members of my family, my parents and eight siblings, were in Brady's Bend. I was away, attending summer school at Penn State. After hearing about the disaster on the radio the following morning, I called home. My mother answered and said, "Brady's Bend is no more."

ACKNOWLEDGEMENTS

My inspiration and energy to undertake this project was made possible due to the encouragement and contributions of many, most especially those who volunteered for interviews, provided advice or donated materials. Thank you to my community of supporters!

A special acknowledgement goes to Brady's Bend Township for providing access to its building for interviews.

An extra special thanks goes to those who provided their family's collections of photos, scrapbooks and newspaper clippings.

Interviewees of Families and Intimate Friends of Those Who Died

Note: Many interviewees donated or loaned their family collections of photos, scrapbooks and newspaper clippings.

Tina Custer Sullivan
Patty (McConville) DeBiasio
Joe and Lois Fink
Jeanne (Potts) Guy
Deborah (Kaufman) Hertweck
Randy A. Hertweck
Mike and Glenda Kaufman
Dan and Paulette Lege
Bill Markel
Susan McCrea
Cheryl Pistorius
Barry Robinson

Interviewees

Note: Many interviewees donated or loaned their family collections of photos, scrapbooks and newspapers clippings.

Monica Andreassi
Shirley Andreassi
Silvio Andreassi
Helen Bartoe
Jeanie Bergman
Bruce and Dianne Bly
Harry Bortmes
Bill Campbell
Terry A. Campbell
David M. Cassesse
Dennis C. Cogley
James L. Curran
Joseph M. Curran
Florence B. DeBacco
Catherine P. Downing
Ernie J. Early
Richard H. Hall
Janice Hamburg
Chris Henderson
James R. Hillwig Jr.
Wade Ion
James King Sr.
Rodney King
Marilyn Magnini
James A. Martin
Kelly Jo (Tascarella) McNaughton
Amy (Kusick) Miller
Karen E. (Olszak) Nee
James A. Olszak
Jeff and Sue Olszak
John M. Olszak
Joseph P. Olszak
Luanne E. Olszak
Tim Patsy
Phillip J. Pezzuti
Harold (Corky) Robinson
Timothy E. Robinson
Mary Ronge
Andrew J. and Karen L. Seybert
Joseph M. Seybert
Thomas A. Seybert
Clifton Sigworth
John D. Slick
Ann E. Stanley
Jill (Kusick) Stimac
Matt Switzer

Reviewers

Stephen Bratkovich
Angelique Burns
Joseph Curran
Brody Daerr
John and Holly Dzemyan
Sean Luce
Emily Miller
James Olszak
Nehal Palan
Martha Perry
Lenora Ramirez-Wildman
Madyson Trama

Technical and Professional Advisors and Researchers

Alex Bond, Alex Bond Photography
Joanna Campbell-Totin, *Butler Eagle*
Werner C. Loehline, PE, PLS, DWRE, University of Pittsburgh, Swanson School of Engineering
Carly T. Lough, Senior Collections Archivist, Senator John Heinz History Center
Sheila Markel, Brady's Bend Township
Dr. Nancy McCabe, PhD, Director of the University of Pittsburgh at Bradford Writing Center
Bill Petrucci, PE civil engineer
Jenna (Buechele) Rupert, Buechele Funeral Home and Cremation Services
Thomas A. Seybert, PhD engineering hydrology
Beth A. Tallentire, Communications Office Coordinator, *Catholic Accent*

Donors of Family Collections

Vincent L. Bartoe
Tim Boltz
Vic and Sharon DeBacco
Mike Hall
Diane McClaine Miskiel
Andrew J. Olszak
Joni (King) Steiner
Vicki Steiner
Marylin Kay Weibel

Introduction

THE POWER OF WATER

Imagine a wine bottle cork in a shallow puddle of water, serene and soothing. A gentle rainstorm shifts it back and forth like it is slow dancing with an invisible partner. The patter of the raindrops creates the dancers' rhythm. Now, imagine that gentle rainstorm transforming into a downpour, or a rain that is falling so hard that it seems to burst from the sky. The cork would fly beyond the puddle, following whatever crazy path the water took. Consider if the puddle was a creek and the cork was someone's home, all the stuff they keep in their yards and on their porches, their cars, mature trees, upturned pavement, bridge decks and railroad trestles. What if the cork was a person?

On August 14, 1980, in Brady's Bend, Pennsylvania, a catastrophic rain event created a flash flood, reducing people and their property to a nightmare of flying corks. Walls of water turned homes and anything that wasn't tied down into crazed corks, careening forward until they disintegrated or were blocked by immovable obstacles or tangles of debris.

Although more than forty years have passed, the memories and emotions of those who experienced the flood remain vivid and raw. Communities that surrounded Brady's Bend were impacted, but the destruction was most horrific along the last three miles of the Sugar Creek in the Brady's Bend corridor, where the nine people lost their lives. After cleanup and restoration, damages to public and private property were estimated to cost more than $12 million ($46 million today).

Brady's Bend is a place that means a lot to me. I grew up there. This chronicle of the 1980 flood started as an offshoot of a family memoir. I talked with all eight of my siblings about their childhoods, including their experience with the flood. Their stories were so compelling that my memoire's copy editor, writer Dr. Nancy McCabe, the director of the

University of Pittsburgh at Bradford's Creative and Professional Writing Program, encouraged me to consider writing a book. Bouncing the idea off a couple of others who had experienced the flood, I discovered a great deal of interest and excitement—so much so that very quickly I had more than sixty people willing to let me record their stories.

While I started with the idea of chronicling a historic event, my research revealed how common catastrophic thunderstorms, and their resulting floods are along the more-than-two-thousand-mile-long Appalachian corridor. Reading through reports and viewing documentaries revealed that survivors often use the same words to describe their experiences.

I learned that the stories of Brady's Bend survivors could be the stories of any other community's flood survivors. Watching West Virginia Public Broadcasting's documentary of the state's 2016 flood, I found myself thinking that I could replace Greenbrier County with Brady's Bend and John Wyatt (a local Greenbrier County resident who rescued several residents) with Tom Seybert (a local Brady's Bend resident who rescued several residents). Even the description of the Greenbrier storm by its residents resonated with déjà vu. Their words were similar if not identical to those from Brady's Bend: "A record amount of water rushed down the hillsides, affecting the valleys….It came up so fast that it went from my ankles to my knees when walking from my kitchen to living room….By the time I realized I needed to get out, it was too late….It caused total annihilation."[1]

I also discovered that documenting a community's traumatic experience inspires families to share their histories. During my interviews, my efforts to document this significant event inspired parents and grandparents to share their stories with younger family members who knew little if anything about the flood.

Married for fifty-three years, Dan and Paulette Lege are the kind of couple who comfortably finish each other's sentences, saying the exact same words at the exact same time. When transcribing their recording, I often chuckled as I replayed sections to see why my transcriber had so badly screwed up the translation. It was because they so often spoke with one voice. Smart technology still has a lot of work to do to translate the beauty of such in-sync partners' conversations. Although we met through FaceTime, Dan and Paulette offered an ease that made me feel I could sink into their couch with a warm cup of tea to talk about the still-painful circumstances of Dan's youngest sister, Carol's, death.

After this conversation and others, I realized that families were telling their family members about my project. For younger members, it was a time for them to learn more about an important part of their family history. In Dan and Paulette's case, it was their fourteen-year-old grandson, Chase's, response that moved me; he wanted to know more about his great-aunt's story, his grandparents' story.

Chase and his older brother Brody knew some about their great-aunt Carol, who, at age twenty-two, was returning to her family home after getting her apartment ready for her second year of teaching at Union School District in Rimersburg, Pennsylvania. By the end of her first year, Carol had become a beloved high school business teacher. Entering Brady's Bend the night of August 14, 1980, Carol and her boyfriend, Calvin Deemer, sought safety from the rising waters at Elrick "Elick" and Bertha "Birch" Custer's home, where Betty Kaufman, on her way home from playing bingo, had also stopped. Carol, Calvin, Betty, Elick, Birch and Elick and Birch's endearing two-year-old grandson, Jerry Potts Jr., were at the house when it was swept off its foundation and destroyed.

Today, Tina (Custer) Sullivan lives in Heath, Texas. She is Elick and Birch's great-niece. She was eighteen at the time of the flood. In a few weeks, she would be leaving East Brady (Brady's Bend's neighboring town) for college in Pittsburgh, Pennsylvania. She had the world by the tail. She and her sensible mother, Betty, worked at Brady's Bend Hotel (Tony's, a bar, restaurant and occasional hotel). Tony's provided employment for many youths, me included. Betty was a bartender with a dry sense of humor and a willingness to play along. Her customers loved her. Tina cooked and served, helping Tony's wife, Thelma, in the kitchen. Tina, Betty and many others were at Brady's Bend Hotel that night for the entire harrowing experience.

During my Zoom conversation with Tina, she combined a joyful energy with serious reflection: "I look back at this, and I think that it made such an impact on me. And it's funny because I never told this story. I have two kids. I have a husband. Brian and I have been married for, gosh, thirty-some years. My daughter Bella is twenty-two, and my son, Micah, is gonna be twenty. Believe it or not, I never told them about this."

Tina said that when she talked with her children about her rural upbringing, they weren't interested. It bored them. When she told heartfelt stories, they looked at her like she was crazy. Yet when she mentioned the flood to her daughter, she said, "Wait, what? I never knew this!" Her daughter was intrigued—so much so that she insisted her mother show her pictures and share more of her experience.

Beyond families sharing their histories, individuals' stories of the Brady's Bend flood built a fuller picture of survival across the Sugar Creek's path. Single accounts fit into a larger whole. Large and small acts of heroism combined with plain luck played a part in the lives of so many.

It's tragic when anyone dies in a natural disaster, but something about the loss of children, like two-year old Jerry Potts Jr., is unbearably heartbreaking.

Another child, Amy Robinson, the four-year-old daughter of Wilson "Butch" and Betty Ellen Robinson, was with her parents that night. They all drowned.

We know that Butch and Betty Ellen were doting parents with a strong sense of family. Butch and his two brothers' and their wives' (Paul and Dolores', and Pete and Elinor's) homes were side by side. Sisters (Dolores and Elinor) had married brothers. Paul's eighteen-year-old son, Barry, his wife and their nine-month-old son lived in a mobile home behind Paul. Betty Ellen's parents lived in the next house down. That section of Brady's Bend was contentedly inhabited by the Robinson clan.

Butch and Betty Ellen had a sixteen-year-old son, and when Amy came along, she was unexpected but greatly wanted. With sandy-colored hair and green eyes, she was her parents' delight. Her mother took her everywhere; a favorite place was high school football games.

While they believed leaving their house would be their escape to higher ground, dreadful bad luck blocked the Robinson truck from moving forward another ten yards to safety. A car had stalled ahead of them. That driver was nearly washed away when he lost his footing while getting out of his car. Two others who were escaping from the storm saved his life.

The story of the Robinsons is the story of several others: those ahead of them, across from them, behind them and on the hillsides above them. None of those storytellers viewed the night from the same vantage point. None of the storytellers knew the extensiveness of others' accounts for not only the Robinsons but for so many others along Sugar Creek's three-mile stretch between its entry to Brady's Bend and confluence at the Allegheny River.

Many of Brady's Bend's storytellers retained powerful emotions about the flood: sorrow for death and overwhelming loss, acknowledgement of the devastation and others' near-death experiences, and recognition of the goodness of all those who helped. Recalling that night was a powerful experience; at least two interviewees reached out afterward to tell me that our conversation had elicited dreams of the flood. That event had become a benchmark for their lives' most terrifying experiences and most impactful traumas.

This chronicle paints a broader picture of the community of Brady's Bend, what caused the storm and the area's survival, recovery and resilience. What happened reflects a larger pattern of destructive storms across the Appalachians. The experience in Brady's Bend could be replaced by numerous other towns that have suffered through similar storms and floods.

Whether you have a connection to the Appalachian region or to Brady's Bend, appreciate a story about hardship and survival or are curious about the impact of floods and other natural disasters to communities, property, businesses and people's emotional well-being, this story is for you.

1

A BIRD'S-EYE VIEW

Like many rural communities, Brady's Bend has a rich history originating with the European immigration of the 1700s and 1800s. That history made the Brady's Bend community what it was in 1980 and is today.

Several of the elements of the thunderstorm that occurred on August 14, 1980, were not unique to Brady's Bend, situated at Pennsylvania's northwestern edge of the central Appalachian region. The Appalachian Mountains have seen some of the largest rainfall accumulations in less than six hours in the world. A world record was set in 1942 in Smethport, Pennsylvania, which saw nearly thirty-one inches of rain in less than five hours.

The rugged and complex terrain (steep slopes, deep valleys, rivers and streams) contribute to some whopper thunderstorms, with catastrophic flooding across the central Appalachian region.[2] Recent headlines reveal flood-causing thunderstorms across that region: 2024 in Oxford, Connecticut[3]; 2022 in eastern Kentucky[4]; and 2016 in West Virginia.[5]

Brady's Bend: A History

As the crow flies, Brady's Bend sits a little more than forty miles northeast of the city of Pittsburgh, along the northwestern perimeter of the Appalachian Plateau. The municipality is named for Captain Samuel Brady; the township and its name were formalized in 1845.

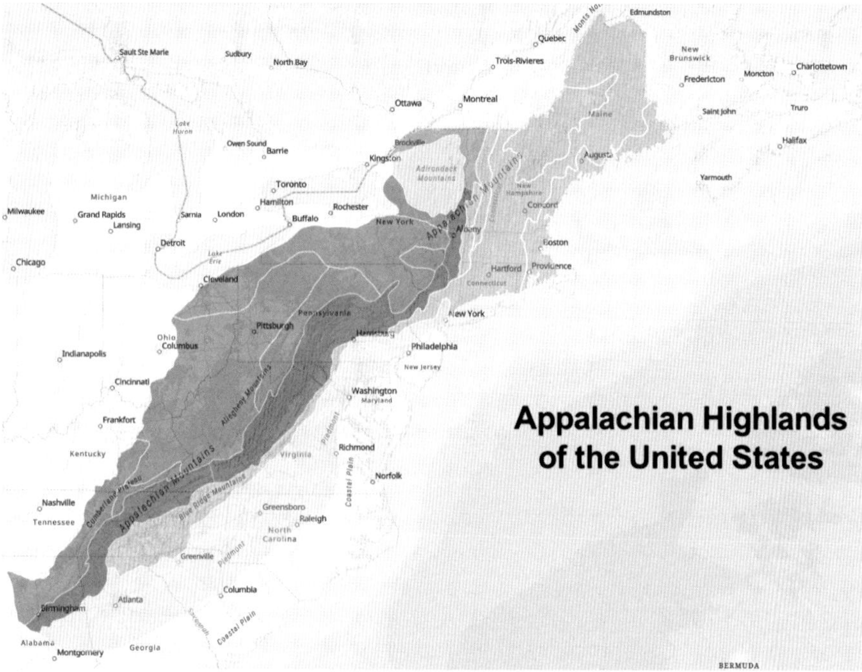

The top three world record-setting thunderstorms occurred in western Pennsylvania's Appalachian corridor (Smethport, Redbank and Johnstown, Pennsylvania). Brady's Bend sits near the center of that area. *Deanrah, Wikimedia Commons, https://commons.wikimedia.org/w/index.php?curid=136631752.*

Like many of Pennsylvania's rural communities that were populated by European settlers in the late 1700s, Brady's Bend was a backwoods community that evolved slowly until its heyday in the mid- to late 1800s. Those glory days were galvanized by natural resources—bituminous coal fueled furnaces used to make iron ore and oil from its first industry boom.

Brady's Bend is where "America first achieved independence from British iron by demonstrating the use of Pennsylvania's coke [a gray, hard, and porous coal-based fuel with a high carbon content] for smelting."[6] The first iron rails made west of the Alleghenies came from Brady's Bend.

The Great Western Iron Company was incorporated in 1839. Abundant deposits of bituminous coal in the western part of Pennsylvania provided coke that fueled the iron industry's early blast furnaces. Several failed attempts in iron manufacturing in the United States led many to dismiss the Great Western Iron Company's plan. Although the company went bankrupt in 1844 after incurring heavy expenses for construction and labor, several of its investors bought and reorganized it as the Brady's Bend Iron Company.

Brady's Bend railroad station, circa the turn of the twentieth century. *Janice Hamburg.*

The iron company's success over the next few decades was fueled by the demand for rails as the railroad expanded west. By 1873, the industry had collapsed, and Brady's Bend and the surrounding communities' population of five thousand had decreased to four hundred by the end of the century.[7]

A 1904 edition of *The Pennsylvania Magazine* highlighted Brady's Bend's former prominence in the production of iron rails that were shipped in barges along the region's river network—the Allegheny and Ohio Rivers from Pittsburgh to Cincinnati, respectively—to their ultimate destinations in the Midwest and the eastern United States.[8]

Despite the Great West Iron Company's bankruptcy, it effectively mastered the use of coke for smelting. The process succeeded mainly due to founders' foresight in "the importation of large numbers of Welsh, Cornish, English and Belgian workmen, skilled in every branch and detail of iron manufacture."[9] The iron ore remnants from two of the earliest blast furnaces still sit side by side along Sugar Creek, near Brady's Bend Township's building.

During the oil boom of the 1860s–90s, prospectors' and investors' exploration began in earnest in the Brady's Bend, Armstrong County area.[10] One active well (of at least seventy-five in the township) pumped as much as one thousand gallons of oil a day. "During the first 15 years of the oil industry Warren, Crawford, Venango, Clarion, Butler, and Armstrong counties furnished approximately 90 percent of the crude oil supply in the world. Nearby Emlenton was reputed to have more millionaires per capita (seven in a population of 1,400) than any other city in the world." When

Brady's Bend industry, 1873. *Janice Hamburg.*

The remains of two Brady's Bend iron ore furnaces. *Janice Hamburg.*

Inventor Andrew J. Seybert and his wife, Matilda "Tillie," circa 1918. *Joseph Seybert.*

the price of oil dropped from twenty dollars a barrel in 1859 to fifty cents a barrel in 1874, the oil industry followed the decline.[11]

In the 1980 phonebook for Brady's Bend, you discover that many family surnames and names of local places are inherited from early settlers, entrepreneurs, investors and inventors: Barnhart, Campbell, Crawford, Donaldson, Forringer, Frazer, Henry, Hicks, Hooks, Jennings, Kemmerer, King, McClaine, Mildren, Phillips, Queen, Seybert, Summerville, Templeton, Walley, Wiles and Wolcott. The Seyberts were especially entrepreneurial. In the late 1800s and early 1900s, at least two Brady's Bend Seyberts held patents. In 1883, Harvey F. Seybert patented a pick, and from 1893 to 1929, Andrew J. Seybert held the patents for a wrench, a running gear for motor vehicles and warp-beams for looms.

Like in many rural communities, in Brady's Bend, direct and indirect descendants have created a web of family networks rooted from those settlers of the early 1900s. Today, local heritage remains primarily European: 40 percent German, 18 percent Irish, 17 percent English and 10 percent Italian, with a smattering of Polish, Scottish, French and Norwegian.[12]

Although Brady's Bend population rebounded some in the 1900s, it never fully recovered from the late 1800s. According to the U.S. Census Bureau, the 1980 population was 1,124 and had declined by 30 percent to 784 by 2020.

Covering 12.61 square miles (one-third the size of Disney World), Brady's Bend's rural setting is in striking contrast to the 2020 population density (people per square mile) of more urbanized areas, like the city of Pittsburgh, with 5,487, versus Brady's Bend's 59. Even more, for every 59 people in that square mile, it's safe to say that the overwhelming majority are related to each another through blood or marriage. The typical six degrees of separation quickly becomes one degree in Brady's Bend. If you live there, you are related in some way to your neighbors and friends.

THE FEATURES OF THE LAND AND WATER

Watersheds

Watersheds are a big deal when it comes to floods. When it rains or the snow melts, water that doesn't evaporate or isn't absorbed into the ground flows toward drains, gutters, ditches, hillside ridges and streams, and then it flows on to larger bodies of water, like rivers, lakes and oceans. Water that feeds a specific stream is part of a defined watershed, where the law of gravity moves water downhill, with steeper terrain increasing its force and speed.

In the shape of a maple leaf, the Brady's Bend Watershed is called Sugar Creek, which is also the name of its main creek. Originating slightly east of Kepple's Corners, a crossroad on two-lane State Route 68 (SR 68) and SR 268, the six-and-a-half-mile-long creek travels through the small community of Kaylor before it enters Brady's Bend a little beyond its halfway point and finally dumps into the Allegheny River. The entire watershed encompasses 11,207 acres.[13]

Amid its rolling hills and narrow valleys, Sugar Creek is fed by six tributaries (Long Run, Pine Run, Holder Run, Cove Run, Hart Run and Whiskey Run). Each of these six tributaries is fed by an extensive web of smaller drainages within the hillside topography. Twisting and turning along SR 68, Sugar Creek, or one of its tributaries, crosses beneath highway bridges fifteen times before meeting the river. The creek winds

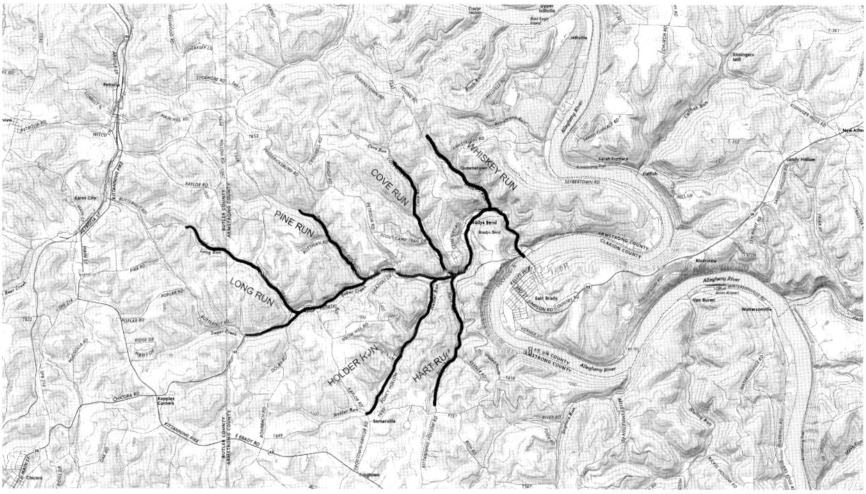

Top: Sugar Creek Watershed. *"How's My Waterway," U.S. EPA.*

Bottom: A topographic map of Sugar Creek and its tributaries. *USGS Topographic Maps.*

back and forth through the community on both sides of the roadway, with the volume of water building as each tributary enters the main drainage. "Normally meandering Sugar Creek reaches a summertime size of six feet wide and six inches deep."[14]

Pennsylvania's Appalachian Topography

Driving from Pittsburgh to Philadelphia along the Pennsylvania Turnpike gives you a good feel for how rolling hills turn into higher mountains and then flatten out beyond Lancaster. Anyone who has driven the turnpike in the winter also knows that sunshine on either side of the state might easily turn into a blinding snowstorm across the Appalachian Mountain range from Somerset to Bedford. Weather within the Appalachians is unpredictable during both the summer and winter. The highest point within that range in Pennsylvania is Mount Davis, south of Somerset.

The Allegheny Mountains and Allegheny Plateau are along the western part of the Appalachian Mountains, extending through Pennsylvania. Their terrain is rugged, with steep slopes and deep valleys, laced with a network of creeks and rivers. As a matter of fact, those networks established American industry as a powerhouse with nature-made routes for transporting people and products. According to a Wikipedia entry on western Pennsylvania, the Allegheny and Monongahela Rivers meet in Pittsburgh to form the Ohio River, which flows 981 miles southwest to the Mississippi River. Since the start of the U.S. Industrial Revolution, the juncture of the Allegheny and Monongahela Rivers has been a gateway to the interior of the continent from the east.[15]

An outdoor recreationist and hunter's paradise, Brady's Bend sits within the Allegheny Mountains, which are a portion of the larger Appalachian Mountains. As part of that mountain chain, Brady's Bend's topography includes steep rolling hills with narrow valleys. Streams and roadways wind amid those valleys.

Sugar Creek and its tributaries can be seen running along valley floors surrounded by steep adjacent hillsides. On the previously presented topography map, notice where the squiggly (or contour) lines are close together. The closer the lines are, the steeper the hillside. In places where contour lines create a V, there is a ridge. There are lots of ridges between Pine Run and Cove Run and then between Cove Run and Whiskey Run. Those ridges make great troughs and amplify how quickly water flows off hillsides and increases its force based on the volume of water that accumulates during its journey. These ridges and the steep hillsides played important roles in amplifying the impact of the 1980 flood.

Catastrophic Thunderstorms

The Appalachian Mountain corridor and Allegheny Mountains are noted for catastrophic thunderstorms that are world-record-setting because of their intensity over a short period. Mentioned previously, Smethport, Pennsylvania's, 1942 whopper storm dumped nearly thirty-one inches of rain in less than five hours. Not far away, two other Pennsylvania thunderstorms broke records for short-term rainfall in that same Appalachian corridor. The 1996 Redbank Creek storm dropped over nine inches of rain in less than twelve hours, and the 1977 Johnstown storm produced nearly twelve inches of rain during an eight-hour period. All three storms consisted of multicellular thunderstorms that moved southeastward from Lake Erie through western Pennsylvania. All three had observations of heavy lightning concentrations within a topography of steep hillsides with lots of ridges.[16] All resulted in world record–setting thunderstorm events.

What happened in Brady's Bend is part of a larger pattern in the Appalachian corridor: short, intense periods of rainfall with lots of lightning and catastrophic flooding with lots of damage. The Brady's Bend flood represents a microcosm of other floods along the Appalachian corridor. What I learned during my research validated stories from Brady's Bend observers, as there were eerily similar tales from those who had experienced other record-breaking thunderstorms.

Consider Tom Seybert's story from August 14, 1980, in Brady's Bend. Tom is one of fifteen Seybert siblings and the grandson of inventor Andrew J. Seybert. In 1980, Tom worked for a civil engineering firm, R.B. Shannon and Associates (consulting engineers), in Kittanning, Pennsylvania, having recently graduated with a master of science degree in civil engineering with an emphasis in hydraulics and hydrology. Eventually, Tom would get a doctorate degree in engineering hydrology and have an admirable career as a professor at Penn State University's Wilkes-Barre campus.

When I interviewed Tom, I knew he had taught at Penn State. Upon learning his specialty was hydrology, I immediately thought, "He knows water! What an amazing resource!" Part of my career involved translating civil engineers' technical language into something the average person could understand. I quickly learned that besides being gifted mathematicians, engineers have a fondness for exactness. In that, Tom didn't disappoint. His timetable of events during the flood was so exact that I asked how he was so sure of the times.

The evening of the flood, after his workday at R.B. Shannon and Associates, Tom went to his family business, arriving when the shop closed around 8:00 p.m. He was working on his sister's car, and he was paying attention to the clock because he did not plan to stay after 10:00 p.m. He wanted to get home early enough to get some sleep and be ready for work the next day.

When the rain started around 9:00–9:15 p.m., Tom noted the time. After that, he gauged the time based on his movements; he knew approximately how much time each task took, and most of them didn't take very long.

Tom's story of what happened reminded me of a similar story from the 1942 Smethport storm. A curious farmer saw the intensity of the rainfall and wondered how fast it was falling. The farmer placed an empty milk pail in his yard. As he returned to the porch, he heard the clock strike 10:00 a.m. He then watched the pail and clock closely, and in five minutes, the milk pail was full.[17] His pail had captured six and a half inches of rain in ten minutes.

Rather than a milk pail, Tom had a bucket. It was a bucket that he used to fill his dog's water bowl with fresh water. Lace was a German Shepherd that was kept outside overnight to deter theft at the business. Tom had filled the water bowl earlier that evening and inadvertently left the empty bucket outside. While the rain started somewhere between 9:00 and 9:15 p.m., it subsided around 10:10 p.m. Tom estimated that it rained hardest for forty minutes of that hour. He went outside and noticed that the depth of the surface runoff coming off the paved driveway/parking area in front of the north side of the garage. It was close to two inches deep. Tom said, "That was astounding. That depth of runoff is rarely seen. It was headed directly toward Hart Run, a stream that runs within ten feet of the west side of the garage and the front driveway edge."

Tom walked to the bank of Hart Run, and it was running about two feet deep, about one-third full. As he walked upstream along the bank, he saw his three-gallon bucket. It was filled with rainwater. It had rained at least ten inches in about forty minutes. His concern intensified. He knew what was to follow would be big.

During my interviews, three others mentioned the depth of the runoff. Each was on a different hillside or part of Brady's Bend. Twenty-three-year-old Bruce Bly, one of the eight Bly brothers, lived in Millionaire Row—a row of six duplexes built as company housing by the Pittsburgh Limestone Company in the first half of the 1900s. Bruce and most of the residents of Millionaire Row crossed SR 68 to get to higher ground on the hillside. Worried about his brother, whose house was one hundred yards farther down Sugar Creek, Bruce walked along the hillside to find a location where he could get a glimpse of his brother's house. He said, "I noticed there were different places where I was walking, where the water coming down off the hill was running over my boots. It was coming down off the hillside that hard."

My twenty-year-old-brother, Jim Olszak, was at St. Patrick's Church in Brady's Bend on an errand for our grandmother, who was the church's housekeeper. When Jim realized the severity of the rain, he knew he needed to hurry home to save our pregnant bloodhound that was kenneled in a field across from our house. At first, he tried to drive home but turned back when the water got so high that his car started to float. Backtracking, he parked at the church. A natural woodsman and hunter, he climbed the hillside. He noted that the runoff was ankle-deep no matter where he stepped. Looking back, he saw his car float away. He wasn't surprised. The dog presented bigger worries than the loss of his car. He was about half a mile from our home. He remembers severe lightning making his hillside hike in the darkness easier.

Joe Curran, who lives in the middle of Brady's Bend, has a home that sits about thirty feet above SR 68. During the storm, he watched his father walk up a gravel road to his house. His father had on his four-buckle Arctics (a black rubber boot with four buckles evenly placed up the front). The runoff was up to his dad's third buckle, at least six inches deep, and the gravel road that meets SR 68 was flowing like a river.

In 1980, there was no formal rain gauge for Brady's Bend. Rainfall measurements were gathered from nearest rain gauges or informal reports. Today, the closest gauge is in Rimer, Pennsylvania (9.25 miles south of Brady's Bend along the Allegheny River). A 1984 report completed for the U.S. Geological Survey titled "Storm-Induced Slope Movements at East Brady, Northwestern Pennsylvania" describes the August 1980 storm's debris avalanche and other slope movements along a steep hillside that faces the Allegheny River toward the town of East Brady. The paper noted that the area was subjected to more than 5 inches of rain, and the town of Brady's Bend along Sugar Creek was the most severely affected community. The thunderstorm began about 8:00 p.m. and became intense between 9:00 p.m. and 10:00 p.m. The rainfall was the heaviest ever experienced by several long-term residents.[18] A farmer's informal rain gauge (on Queenstown Road along Whiskey Run) was used by this study to document the amount of rainfall.

The heavy rain occurred where two violent thunderstorms met. One storm moved into Pennsylvania during the afternoon and then stalled east to west through central Pennsylvania. A second storm came from north to south. This second storm met the first that night in Brady's Bend. The net effect of these two storms stalling in Brady's Bend was rainfall intensity and duration like no one had seen before. Making matters worse, well-above-normal rainfall in western Pennsylvania for July and early August meant that the ground was already saturated.[19] Like a sponge that is full, the ground was unable to absorb more water.

The 1980 summer weather was so unusual, it made local headlines. According to meteorologist Lou Giordano from the National Weather Service, there were between fifteen and twenty tornadoes that touched down in western Pennsylvania in June and early July. There were twenty-eight storms, while twenty is normal. There were twenty-seven flash flood warnings and watches, the most since the summer of 1975, when there were thirteen. The summer of 1980 was the third rainiest ever in Pittsburgh (the closest city to Brady's Bend).[20] Between 1919 and 1977, the average precipitation from June to August was 11.43 inches in East Brady, Pennsylvania (Brady's Bend's neighboring community).[21] In the summer of 1980, the rain total over the same period was more than 16 inches.[22]

The deluge of rain on August 14 was estimated to be over five inches by the Queenstown farmer's gauge, yet there is no reason to doubt Tom Seybert's bucket indicating at least ten inches at his location.

According to the U.S. National Oceanic and Atmospheric Administration (NOAA), experiencing 3.5 inches of rain in one hour and 10.9 inches in twelve hours is likely to happen only once in one thousand years. How common is it to see 10 inches of rain in forty minutes—a storm likely to occur once every ten thousand years? Whatever it's called, it was a beyond believable amount of water that assaulted the 17.5-square-mile Sugar Creek Watershed that night.[23] Within that hour of heaviest rainfall, "the creek had risen to the road, in another 15 minutes it went three feet higher and then to a depth of 12 feet in some places."[24] In some areas, the creek expanded from its normal 6 feet to 40 forty wide.[25]

I asked Tom Seybert and Bill Petrucci (a civil engineer whom I had worked with for over a decade) to help me put that quantity of water into perspective. They came up with this: 10 inches is 0.8333 feet, so 0.8333 feet over 11,207 acres, with 43,560 square feet per acre, means there was 406,800,000 cubic feet of water. That's 3,042,900,000 gallons, the equivalent of 508,500 average backyard swimming pools that are 10 by 20 feet and

4 feet deep. Imagine over 500,000 pools emptied in Brady's Bend in forty minutes, roaring down hillsides, into tributaries and then on to Sugar Creek, overflowing and carrying debris everywhere.

A handful of survivors were convinced that other bodies of water in the area had broken free (from the added stress of the storm), intensifying the runoff—beaver dams atop the hillside, two ponds near Kaylor used by the Western Allegheny Division of Bessemer Railroad for refilling their steam engines or an abandoned mineshaft full of water.

My brother Jim Olszak, a retired gamelands maintenance supervisor, has released and observed water from numerous large beaver dams. He said that the water from even the largest beaver dam would not be significant enough to make any real impact. Regarding the railroad retention ponds, because of the elimination of steam engines, by 1948, both ponds were no longer in use and had been removed or filled in. Either way, railroad historian Joe Curran noted, "You could have dynamited both ponds simultaneously and unless I told you that it was happening, you would never notice the water level increase in Sugar Creek." Finally, although there were a handful who believed that the release of a water-filled mineshaft worsened the flooding, the largest active mine, Brady's Bend Limestone Mine, was toured immediately after the flood, and nothing was found. Dan Lege said that shortly after his sister's drowning, his father received a call inviting him to join others in suing the mines for a breakage. Dan's father declined, saying that a suit "wouldn't bring Carol back." Throughout my research, I found no record of any suit ever occurring or any mention of mine shafts' discharge.

Interestingly, among all types of natural disasters (earthquakes, wildfires, volcanoes, drought), according to a 2022 report by the Pew Charitable Trusts, "Flooding continues to be the most common and costly natural disaster in the country, with flood-related disasters. From 2000 through 2021, at least one flooding event was reported in the country on 8 out of every 10 days."[26] That's a lot!

If you follow national news, you are familiar with flood event headlines. Whether you were in Brady's Bend in 1980 or not, the odds that you or someone you know has experienced a flood are high. And although hurricanes are getting stronger, more intense and harder to predict (nearly doubling in the last forty years), "The NOAA Storm Events Database shows that even during the June–November Atlantic hurricane season, the majority of days with flooding were not reported as associated with tropical cyclones but involved other events such as flash floods, lakeshore floods, and seiches (significant waves typically driven by strong winds or rapid changes in atmospheric pressure)."[27]

The power of the water in Brady's Bend on August 14, 1980, was so significant that a minimum of fifty thousand tons of loose earth was washed from the cliff-like slopes abutting the Allegheny River. About one-quarter of that entered the river.[28] To put this in perspective, the average triaxle coal truck hauls around twenty-two tons of material. Meaning 2,273 trucks would be needed to move fifty thousand tons of material, with 568 of them dumping their load in the river. Another "wow" to the significance of the storm.

Beyond the river-facing hillside, storm survivors saw evidence of landslides throughout Brady's Bend, and in some cases, these slides threatened their lives. Compounding the landslides was the soil from runoff that created a nightmare of mud everywhere.

2

AUGUST 14, 1980

To best understand what happened on the night of August 14, 1980, in Brady's Bend, one should follow the last portion of Sugar Creek as it enters Brady's Bend. The following stories of those who experienced the flood will trace the creek from Holder Run (the third of six tributaries in Sugar Creek) over 2.25 miles into the Allegheny River. That's where the bulk of the damage occurred. That's where nine innocent people with full lives and loving families perished.

This part of my narrative is divided into three sections: Upper Brady's Bend (.5 miles), Middle Brady's Bend (1 mile) and Lower Brady's Bend (.75 miles). These are artificial borders that I created to group the experiences of our storytellers in a way that illustrates how the people, topography and watershed impacted what happened that night. The stories come from more than sixty individuals, most of whom were residents at the time. This willing group of interviewees reflects what happened to the entire Brady's Bend community.

Along SR 68, the mile and a half that comes before you enter Upper Brady's Bend is absent of homes. Instead, charming deciduous tree-covered hillsides border the northern side of the highway with railroad tracks on the southern side. Interconnected hillsides continue through the entirety of Brady's Bend, enfolding valleys, widening slightly in Middle Brady's Bend and narrowing dramatically in Lower Brady's Bend.

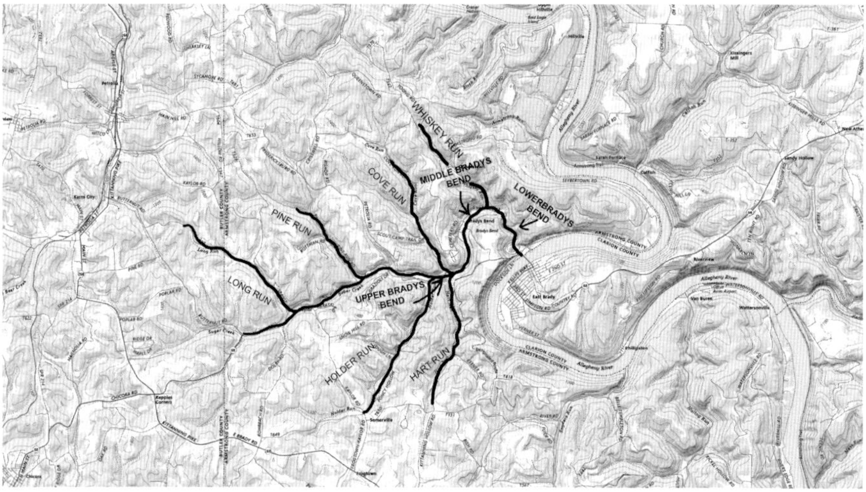

A topographic map of Upper Brady's Bend, Middle Brady's Bend, Lower Brady's Bend. *USGS Topographic Maps.*

In Upper Brady's Bend, housing for approximately fifty families once sat on both sides of the highway. Beyond these neighbors' yards, the hillsides and valleys were natural playgrounds. In one location, six duplexes called Millionaire Row housed twelve families. These households produced a cadre of children who gathered beyond their backyards to meet their friends across the creek in Meatball Stadium. Formerly a U.S. Steel storage area for limestone, Meatball Stadium, in 1980, was a valley floor, large enough for pickup games of any type.

The hillsides around the stadium were state gamelands, dotted with homemade deer stands. During one visit to the stadium, I decided to explore the hillsides instead. While I was climbing an ancient deer stand without checking the stability of its homemade steps, one split. I fell twelve feet and instinctively tried to break my fall with my hand. Instead, I landed on my back with a thump. With my air knocked out, I couldn't breathe. I didn't notice my wrist's compound fracture until I was able to sit up. Like many Brady's Bend children in the 1980s, I had gone off with no adult at hand. No matter where you were in Brady's Bend, unsupervised children played with friends at local gathering spots or explored the hillsides.

Boney dumps, with the discarded spoils from coal mining, were everywhere. Sometimes, they increased the steepness of embankments, covering them with a thin, slippery shale. One favorite dump offered a primitive version of a Slip 'N Slide®. Children started at the top on their haunches, making every effort to avoid being flipped onto their backs as they gathered speed on their way to the bottom. Another dump culminated in a wide flat bottom against the hillside. It became a shale-made shooting range.

Upper Brady's Bend also included three bars, two of them with active kitchens and occasionally rented rooms. After or before work on weekdays, locals gathered to meet friends, have a drink or grab a quick snack and supper. On the weekends, the bars were Brady's Bend's primary source of entertainment.

Other local establishments in Upper Brady's Bend included a beer distributor, a beauty salon, a barbershop, a general store, Seybert's Sunoco garage and Daman Industries machine shop.

In Middle Brady's Bend, another fifty or so single-family homes sat in small clusters along both sides of the highway. This area included three churches (one was the home of the local historical society), a tire shop, an elementary school and Martin's Texaco. The valley is slightly wider in this section compared to Upper Brady's Bend.

Middle Brady's Bend offered the most "entertainment" centers. The elementary school, which sat in the widest part of the valley, had a playground with swing sets, slides, a jungle gym and a merry-go-round. All were old-fashioned, made of metal and full of opportunities for bumps, bruises and, sometimes, broken bones. The equipment offered the epitome of life's hard knocks. Behind the school was an asphalt basketball court. Below the court sat a baseball field used for pickup games and Little League competitions, a popular community gathering place.

Two cemeteries, St. Mary's Catholic and Brady's Bend, sit at the very top of opposing hillsides. Each offers a peek into the past, like the stones of residents who were born in Europe in the 1700s and died in Brady's Bend in the mid-1800s. These historic headstones hint at fascinating stories, like that of Cass and Love Jones, who were born in the mid-1800s. Five of their six children didn't live beyond the age of seven, including one set of twins. Their only surviving child, a son, had one child, Lieutenant John. W. "Bud" Jones of the 753rd Tank Battalion, who died in the line of duty on June 19, 1942, perhaps ending Cass and Love's bloodline.

Another fascinating headstone is that of "Drummer Boy Robt. D. Sutton. Co. D. 62nd Regt. P.V.I 1844–1934." After serving in the Civil War, Robert Sutton lived to the ripe age of ninety.

Continuing beyond Brady's Bend Cemetery, across its hilltop, sat the local garbage dump. Although there may have been laws that required trash to be covered, they were lightly followed in 1980. Whether its visitors were

Brady's Bend Cemetery, Robert Sutton's tombstone. *Andy J. Olszak.*

scavenging for items for possible reuse or shooting bottles, crows or rats for sport, the dump was a happening place.

In both Upper and Middle Brady's Bend, all children played in the creek, catching chubs, minnows, crayfish or water snakes. The creeks also attracted trappers of muskrats and raccoons and those who sought target practice on the Norway rats that thrived on some residents' daily creek dump of raw sewage or trash.

Middle Brady's Bend's valley featured two ponds that were used for winter skating or summer frog hunting. Tram roads, remnants of the industrial past's railway or other transport networks, offered hillside shortcuts to friends' homes or favorite hunting spots.

Compared to that of Upper and Middle Brady's Bend, Lower Brady's Bend's topography changes noticeably. The valley narrows significantly. The creek's incline drops dramatically as it travels to the river. This section is also more sparsely populated. Less than ten homes (one with a flooring business) dotted the roadway until the creek reached the river, where there were a cluster of homes, a gas station and a bar. This section of Brady's Bend is characterized by the sharp snaking turns on SR 68 as it crosses over numerous small bridges.

Sugar Creek

By the time Sugar Creek enters Brady's Bend, it has traveled four miles. Two of its six tributaries (Long Run and Pine Run), with their web of hillside springs and seeps, have emptied into it. While we don't know exactly how many inches of rain poured across the full watershed on August 14, 1980, we know the amount was extraordinary; it swept down hillsides, engorged ridges, sought channels and low points, built momentum and amassed a torrent of debris. By the time the water continued into Brady's Bend, many residents declared they saw a "wall of water three to four feet high" barreling toward them.

Unfortunately, the flood warning system that was put into place in 1977, after the Johnstown's flash flood that killed seventy-six people, failed in Brady's Bend. In each county, volunteers were equipped with radios and other equipment and were on standby when a flood watch was issued. Armstrong County had thirteen such volunteers. The system worked with the National Weather Service. When a watch was issued, volunteers recorded rainfall, and if it was above a specific amount, they reported that total to their coordinator. In turn, the coordinator could directly issue a local flood warning without consulting the National Weather Service. In 1980, John Comey of the Pennsylvania Emergency Management Agency's Harrisburg office said the system worked, but it had its problems. "[It] depends on volunteers. They take vacations, go away and go to sleep at night."[29]

It doesn't seem likely that the dependence on volunteers was the issue on August 14, 1980. The rain came so hard and fast that by the time a volunteer would have measured and reported the rain, the destruction of the flood was already occurring.

Upper Brady's Bend

Driving east, Blue Row Coal Tipple sat on the right about a quarter of a mile before Holder Run, part of the last section of the Bessemer and Lake Erie Railroad system in Brady's Bend. One of its remaining railroad trestles crossed over Holder Run.

Immediately beyond Holder Run sat the first bar (Rocket Hotel) and then Millionaire Row (mentioned earlier, the row of six duplexes was built by the Pittsburgh Limestone Company as company housing and later sold to

Blue Row coal Tipple. *Florence DeBacco.*

residents). The six Millionaire Row duplexes contained twelve households. The story of what happened to those households is garnered from four of those families and another resident from across the road.

Millionaire Row

The first duplex was the home of Jim and Debbie Pezzuti and their baby. Jim's parents, Tony and Thelma Pezzuti, owned Brady's Bend Hotel (Tony's) another one hundred yards down SR 68. Jim worked for nearby Daman Industries (a machine shop that specialized in equipment repair and reconditioning), which was visible from Brady's Bend Hotel at the intersection of Hart Run and SR 68.

In 1980, three shifts covered twenty-four hours, and Jim was working the third, or overnight, shift. While Jim slept before his overnight shift, his youngest brother, Phil (who was twelve at the time), was babysitting. Phil recounted what happened that night.

Attractive and stylish, Debbie was and still is the popular owner and operator of Scissor Magic, a well-known hair salon. That evening, when the shop closed, she headed home. When she arrived, she saw the threat of the rising water and immediately retrieved their dog that was tied up in the yard below the house.

A Millionaire Row neighbor across the road, Harry Bortmes (a man who typically preferred his independence and solitude), and his wife were watching the water rise. Their home sat slightly higher than SR 68 and was staying dry. Sensing the growing threat to Millionaire Row residents, Harry went into action. He telephoned the Pezzutis and urged them to seek safety at his house. They agreed. Hurriedly, Harry drove his Blazer through tire-high water to retrieve them.

Phil recalled entering Harry's vehicle. The current took his foot as he stepped from the porch. Some adults on the porch kept him secure. They guided his crossing. With a full vehicle, Harry delivered his passengers to his house. Harry Jr. (who was five at that time) remembers his dad getting the Pezzutis. As he watched from the safety of his home, he recalled hearing an awful crushing sound as five of the six garages behind Millionaire Row were ripped away.

Once he was settled at the Bortmeses', Phil Pezzuti was concerned for his parents and their business; the drop in elevation from Millionaire Row to Brady's Bend Hotel was significant enough that the water would become higher as it moved down Sugar Creek and SR 68.

Millionaire Row residents Bruce Bly and his wife, Dianne, were a local couple turned world travelers. They began dating in their senior year of high school and graduated in 1975. In 1976, Bruce enlisted in the army. They were married in 1977. By 1979, they had lived in Louisiana and then Italy. Then they moved to Brady's Bend, settling in Millionaire Row. Their oldest son, born in Italy, was almost two years old in August 1980.

Bruce joined the U.S. Army Reserves in 1979 and is known for his stalwart service career in the U.S. Army, U.S. Army Reserves and Pennsylvania State Police.

After receiving an alert from neighbors, Bruce moved his family's car away from the creek behind their duplex. Watching the rising water, Bruce and Dianne realized that they needed to retrieve their dog that was chained across the creek. Bruce and a neighbor used a footbridge to cross. When they turned back with the dog, the water was too high to return the way they had come. Cars were already floating between the houses and garages. They worked their way one hundred yards upstream to higher ground. The bridge that crossed the Holder Run tributary and Sugar Creek was crossable. From there, they returned home.

The backside of Millionaire Row, August 15, 1980. *James King Sr.*

By now, Bruce's father had arrived from his hillside home to take the family to safety. Like locals who had grown up in the area, Bruce's father knew the hillside backroads that would allow him to safely enter Upper Brady's Bend. Dianne and the toddler left. Bruce remained to help others.

A few duplexes down were the residences of Joe and Toots King on one side and John and Sis Kusick on the other. Empty nesters who were recently retired, Joe and Toots had raised five children. Now, they had only their dog Muffin. Joe, Toots and Muffin joined others across SR 68, the Millionaire Row gathering spot. Joe told reporters from the *Butler Eagle* (a local newspaper), "It put you in mind of water running into a glass real slow. It just kept coming up and coming up. It was as high as your belt buckle on Route 68."[30]

John and Sis Kusick had seven children; the four youngest were living at home. John was a big man with a big character. Like many men in Brady's Bend, he was a commemorated World War II combat veteran and in every way a survivor. Beyond the war, John survived being shot by another hunter, a ruptured hernia that left his intestines dangling out and a long crawl through the woods with a broken ankle. Sis was the behind-the-scenes backbone of the family. She kept the family engine running smoothly, including keeping all the children in line.

Married at twenty-two years old, their daughter Amy had a five-month-old son. Sis was babysitting while Amy was visiting with cousins. When Amy returned to her parent's home to pick up her baby, her aunt was there. Amy needed sandwich meat for her husband's lunchbox, so her aunt invited her to their house along Cove Run for some extra she had on hand. Amy left the baby with her mother, planning to return shortly. She never made it back that night.

Sis and John's youngest daughter, Jill, was ten at the time. She recalled the adults watching the creek rise until it came down the highway. That's when they decided to seek safety across the highway. Her dad took her mom and the baby first. When he returned, he put Jill and her twin brother under his arms and crossed again. The two older children came as well. As a child, Jill remembers closely watching the adults, especially her parents. They seemed afraid. For her, at ten years old, that meant "it was a bad thing."

Before John and Sis left the house, Amy was on the phone telling Sis that she was trapped in her aunt's home and could not get back. Amy knew that the family planned to cross SR 68, dodging the debris that her mother was describing as it rushed by. While they were talking, phone service was lost. Amy said, "Not knowing if my baby was safe was the most terrifying experience of my life. I don't remember how and when I got to him the next day, but I remember a feeling of crushing anxiety and terror that entire night."

The men from Millionaire Row and Harry Bortmes became a small army, ushering everyone to the other side, including those who were not keen on leaving their home, like the infamous Annie Bucar. An intimidating force, Annie owned and lived in one of the Millionaire Row duplexes. Children gave Annie's yard and flowers a wide berth. Annie was in her seventies at the time, and it took a lot of convincing to get Annie and her visiting brother to leave. Harry Bortmes got a rope and tied it off at his home and then onto a Millionaire Row porch. Harry, known for his strength in manually lowering a transmission into a car, put Annie over his shoulder and carried her through waist-deep water to the other side.

All the men helped other Millionaire Row residents to safely cross. The Bortmeses' home became a shelter for many of those families, and Harry's wife, Phyllis, supplied them with blankets, towels, food and drinks.

Hendersons, Bartoes and Olszaks

Another thirty yards beyond Millionaire Row sat the Henderson house with another cluster of homes across SR 68. One was Helen and Kermit Bartoe's. Neither the Bartoes nor Hendersons made it out of their homes before the water became too swift and high. Both families spent the night on their second floor.

Chris Henderson; his wife, Barb; and their seven-year-old son lived with Chris's seventy-six-year-old father. While preparing a late dinner, Chris heard a loud sound coming from his basement. Upon investigation, he saw water pouring through the basement windows. In less than ten minutes, Chris watched the water rise from the steps on his front porch to four feet in his living room.

As they hurried upstairs, the backdoor burst open, and a railroad tie entered the home and then exited through the opposite door. The refrigerator ping-ponged off the walls in the kitchen. Through the window, he watched logs, railroad ties and cars bounce off the side of his house. Chris said, "The water was a constant roar. My son, Ray, asked if he was going to grow up. We all wondered if the house would stay put."

During the night, the only protection the Hendersons' house had was a slight opening in the valley and flatter terrain, which slowed the current a hair. Although it was a long few hours and one of the Hendersons' kitchen walls was pushed out, their house stayed put.

At the Bartoes's home, the experience was much the same, except that Helen was on her own with the four youngest of their six children (ages eleven to fifteen) and her seventeen-year-old daughter's best friend who was visiting. Helen's husband was at work. Realizing the threat of the water, she had the children quickly gather their new bicycles and place them on the porch. With Helen praying the rosary, they watched from an upstairs window as the water tore off their porch and carried the new bicycles away.

At the intersection of Sugar Creek and Cove Run tributary sat my family's home. The four sisters had a bedroom with a window that faced the creek. My three sisters remembered our parents standing in their bedroom, watching the rising creek with panicked looks on their faces.

After the creek crested its bank and began to lap against the house, our parents said that they had to get out. My sister Pam recalled, "This rain was different. The creek would get high and nearly over the bank at other times. It would even be raging. So, I never thought anything of it, until that night. Mom and dad had to have known it was different. When dad said, 'Get out

Henderson's house, August 15, 1980. *Helen Bartoe.*

Bartoe's house with a missing porch, August 15, 1980. *Helen Bartoe.*

now,' he wasn't messing around. He didn't yell, but I could feel the panic from him and mom."

As the girls put on their shoes, three of my brothers who were already in bed were awakened. The youngest, age eleven, said that he was pulled out of bed and halfway down the steps before he awoke. Another recalled coming downstairs and glancing out the window to see the neighbor's car floating by. While this happened, our brother Jim was on his hillside hike, trying desperately to get to our kenneled dog and our family. It wasn't until the early morning hours that my family would learn of Jim's fate.

Jeff, twenty-two, who worked a midnight shift, was returning to our home from Brady's Bend Hotel. When he arrived, the water was ankle-deep in the driveway. A few minutes later, as my family left the house, the water was above Jeff's knees. The speed at which the water rose increased their urgency.

Jeff wanted to get his and my oldest brother's immaculately restored 1960s Chevelles and every other car to safety. Whether moving those cars would have made any difference, we'll never know—mom's car was blocking them. Rare for her, the keys were not in her car's ignition, and there was no time to go back into the house to retrieve them.

My oldest brother was also worried about saving another car, his Subaru. A mechanical engineer for Koppers Inc., he had participated in an all-day meeting at the corporate headquarters in Pittsburgh. At the end of the day, it was his responsibility to deliver an enlarged framed photo of a resorcinol crystal, one of the company's industrial products, to his Petrolia office. Producing this photo had been an expensive undertaking. That night, the framed photo was in the back of his car.

On the porch, dad directed everyone to grab the hand of the person next to them, forming a human chain to cross the flooding gravel road to the hillside. We had two housedogs. One, a bloodhound, loved water and was famous for underwater rock diving. When he saw the high water, he excitedly dove in. Fortunately, both dogs were leashed. The basset hound was at the back of the line, where she was picked up by the water and began floating away. Terrified, one sister screamed, "She can't swim!" Jeff pulled the dog to safety.

Pam remembers our mother later telling her that as they crossed the roadway, our dad began counting the kids and then screamed, "Where's Pam? Where's Pam?" Our mom, who was nearest him, said, "You are holding her hand!"

John Olszak's Subaru with a framed photograph of resorcinol in the back. *John M. Olszak.*

Olszak's house along Sugar Creek with the hillside (*left*) in the background. *Florence DeBacco.*

Every step toward the hillside was hindered by an intense current and debris bouncing off everyone's legs. They worked their way across the road, linked in a mutually dependent chain, soaking wet with rain. The power of the water was terrifying.

After finally reaching the hillside, they climbed and walked one hundred yards across the hill until they were directly behind my grandparents' trailer. Fortunately, it sat close to the hillside and was partially sheltered from the current by the house above. My brothers descended and entered the trailer. One of them remembers our dad saying that when the water reached the top of the trailer's skirt, they needed to get our grandparents on the hillside. In only minutes, they felt the trailer rock. They had to leave.

My grandmother had been pacing in her nightgown, wondering what to wear. My eternally patient grandfather sat calmly. As part of his rainfall routine, he slowly put on his rubbers that covered only the soles of his shoes. Seeing the senselessness in this act, one of my brothers told him he didn't need them. My brothers led our grandparents out of their trailer and onto the hillside while my dad rushed back to our home to chain our tow truck (for their business, Olszak's Garage) to a telephone pole so it wouldn't be washed away.

Described by each of my siblings, the sound of fast-moving water was "loud, thundering, roaring, raging, sounded like a train going by, you couldn't hear yourself think."

Pam said that the night felt odd because it was lit by the lights in homes and the storm's lightning. She watched the water come off the hillsides and rage through the town. She said, "Where the homes were supposed to be, it was a raging river. It wasn't the yards that we played in and the homes where you'd see porches and whatever. It was like somebody threw a raging river right there."

Amid the sound of raging water was a small community of people on the hillside, yelling, "Are you OK?" While others yelled back, "Yes!" This same community could hear Chris Henderson calling out his upstairs window. No one could reach him now. The Hendersons were trapped. Many began to pray.

As lights shone from houses, everyone experienced the same feeling of awe and horror as they watched cars and other debris flying by and listened to the dreadful sounds of the night.

August 14, 1980

Brady's Bend Hotel

The evening of August 14, 1980, like every Thursday, was Wing Night at Brady's Bend Hotel. Soon to be a freshman at college, Tina Custer wasn't scheduled to work that evening, but co-owner Thelma Pezzuti called her in as kitchen help, believing they would get busy. Because of the day's earlier rains, Thelma's husband had left to make sure his boat was secure on the Allegheny River. He wouldn't be able to make it back that night. Tina's mother, Betty, was tending bar.

Tina was on cloud nine, having shopped that day for dorm room bedding and supplies with her hard-earned savings. It would be her first time leaving home, and she was thrilled to be departing rural East Brady for the city of Pittsburgh. She'd had a full day, so she wasn't keen on working that evening, but when Thelma asked, she figured every dollar counted—the seven or eight dollars she'd make that Thursday night would at least fill her car's gas tank.

More than a dozen customers were in the bar, with four more in the dining room. Kelly Tascarella, Debbie McCanna, her cousin Jackie McCanna and Matt Switzer had been at Debbie's house on Seybertown Road, which runs northeast along the Allegheny River. Hungry, they agreed on wings at Brady's Bend Hotel. A few left in Jackie's stunning new black Trans Am, identical to the one in the Burt Reynolds movie *Smokey and the Bandit*. Debbie drove her equally stunning new T-roof Camaro with the others.

When they arrived, it was sprinkling. As they waited for their order, it began raining harder. Before too long, water was coming in under the dining room's outer door. Thelma brought rags and buckets and asked Kelly and her crew to sop up the water, wring it into the buckets then dump it in the toilet. Thelma didn't know that this was a battle her cooperative customers would not win.

When Thelma returned to the dining room, a few inches of water covered the floor. She announced to all the customers that she thought they needed to go upstairs. Those in the dining room immediately agreed.

Before Kelly left, she decided to prop open the door between the dining room and the bar. As she reached for the door, the exterior dining room door blew open. Behind it was a tidal wave of water that went from Kelly's ankles to her chest in an instant. It slammed the dining room door closed, trapping three of Kelly's fingers in the frame.

Ensnared in the door, Kelly was knocked off her feet. She said, "I kept trying to pull my fingers out and they were stuck in the door, so the wave of water took me under. I knew when to breathe because when I came up, I could see the jukebox lights as I surfaced. When I saw those lights, I knew to take a breath. Then I went back under. The water plunged me under over and over."

Shortly before, neighbors arrived at the bar. They warned patrons of the threat of flooding. Doubtful, the patrons said, "Wait, what?" Everyone knew it was raining, but they didn't want to leave their perches. Tina Custer reflected, "Within minutes, you could hear stuff right outside. The neighbor said, 'Look, this is serious. The water's gonna come in here.' We were shocked because this didn't happen, but everybody agreed, OK, well, maybe we should go upstairs. Can you believe we took time to lock the doors? It didn't make a difference. We didn't turn the lights off, yet we locked the doors."

On the other side of the bar door, Debbie finally turned around from the steps and saw Kelly. She realized what was happening. She ran back and stood Kelly up on her feet, but Kelly remained trapped in the door.

At that point, the people at the bar were desperate to get upstairs, and they had to go through the dining room door. They pushed the door with their shoulders, trying to force it open. It wasn't budging, not with Kelly's fingers stuck in the frame on the other side. They had no clue. They hammered, trying even harder to get the door open. Finally, they rammed the door, and it sprung loose. Kelly's fingers were pulled free. Everyone went upstairs, still unaware that Kelly's (now broken) fingers had been in the frame.

Tina said, "The water was already coming up the steps, so we just ran. Nobody screamed. Nobody was crying. Everybody was shocked. We didn't think it would go higher."

Upstairs, they were horror-struck. They put up the windows and looked out. As patrons watched, they saw the hotel sign above the dining room door dangling from chains out front. Kelly said, "It said, 'Brady's Bend Hotel, spaghetti something.' Another sign hung below and said, 'parking in the rear.' The water was up to 'parking in rear.' The lightning lit up the sky. We could see railroad ties floating in the water, and you knew they were going to hit that old building. And each hit jarred us. It was scary as hell."

Within a few minutes, they went from a pleasant evening out, to a level of denial and disbelief, to racing the rising water to get upstairs. Tina said that when she looked out the window, the water looked like dark ice. The noise of railroad ties hitting the building was unnerving. They watched the little house next door being pummeled by cars, ties and debris. They expected it to loosen from its foundation at any moment.

Brady's Bend Hotel (*left*), Pezzuti's General Store (*right*) and railroad ties settled in front, August 15, 1980. *Tim Patsy*.

A small house next door to Brady's Bend Hotel, August 15, 1980. *Helen Bartoe*.

Their own cars floated behind and beyond the hotel. The intensity of the water's force was astonishing. The entire scene was surreal. For some, their response was as surreal as the scene. Under Thelma's direction, they began ripping sheets into lengths so they could tie everyone together. If they were washed away, they would go as a group.

Two of the Seybertown friends had left before the escape upstairs, before the wall of water hit. Jackie McCanna and Matt Switzer intended to check on Jackie's dad, who lived a quarter mile farther down SR 68. Her dad was home alone. Because he had a prosthetic leg, they wanted to make sure he was safe and turn on his sump pump. They made it twenty yards before they realized their effort was futile.

They were nearly at Seybert's garage when they turned around. That's when they heard Keith Christie, whose car had stalled in front of the Robinson family's. When Keith exited his car, he struggled, slipped and fell. Miraculously, Jackie was close enough to grab Keith's arm and the front of his shirt and pull him up. Matt grabbed his hand and offered to help with the heavy box.

Keith owned an East Brady restaurant and was on his way home. Matt admitted that the sound of the rushing water was deafening. It was a miracle they heard Keith's screams. Keith didn't want to let go of the box. It was heavy and soaked; it was the money and receipts from the day's business. The three rushed to higher ground, to a slightly elevated home across the road. As soon as they were on the porch, Keith latched onto his money box. Together, they watched an incredible scene. Matt said, "At one point the water was hitting the sign on Brady's Bend Hotel and the sign was waving back and forth, and I saw Debbie and Kelly looking out the upstairs window. I called my stepmother from the house and told her, 'I hope I see you.' Then the phone went dead."

Meanwhile, Kelly and Debbie believed that Jackie and Matt had surely drowned. According to Kelly, "We didn't know what happened to them until later. We had no clue because we couldn't see them. We thought they were dead. Debbie kept saying, 'Oh my God, I'm going to have to raise Jackie's younger sister.'"

Meanwhile, Tina was convinced that God had put her there with her mother. As an only child to a single mother, she said it would have been unbearable for her mother to not know at the end of the night that she was safe.

Rodney King and his now-former wife, Monica Andreassi (seven months pregnant with their first child), left Brady's Bend Hotel dining room as the

Monica Andreassi and Rodney King's car a half mile from their escape, August 15, 1980. *Monica Andreassi.*

rain quickened. They were seeking the safety of Rodney's father's home in Millionaire Row. They made it less than twenty yards before their car stalled in the high water. They were stuck, and the pressure of the water wouldn't let them open their car doors. They are alive today because of Tom Seybert. Rodney firmly believes that seven people lived because of Tom: Seybert's garage neighbor Mae, Monica, their three future children and Rodney himself.

"Perhaps the 'happiest victim,' despite the fact that his car was a mile downstream from the original parking spot, was Jack Heils, who was trapped in the Brady's Bend Hotel, where a dozen patrons suddenly found themselves 'waist deep' in water. Resigned to their predicament, Heils and the other patrons accepted the hospitality of their host until the water receded."[31]

Seybert's Sunoco Garage

Earlier, I mentioned Tom Seybert, our hydrology engineer. On August 14, he started working on his sister's car around 8:00 p.m., when his family's garage closed. When the sound of the rain became louder than his orbital sander, he stopped working and looked out the large plate-glass window in the rear of the shop. He saw a continuous sheet of water running off the garage's almost flat roof. The depth of the sheet of water was significant as it crashed to the ground at the base of the window. Tom said,

> *I could not believe the intensity of the rain. All I could hear was rain hitting the garage roof. As I stared at the ceiling in amazement at the noise, a few small leaks started to appear, first dripping, then running full stream in three or four places. I peeked out the windows and saw nothing but rain. Visibility was very limited. I watched in amazement and awe. This was incredible. I had studied the hydrologic aspects of intense rainfall and the following runoff. I knew we would be in for some flooding in the next few hours. I just didn't know how much.*

When the rain subsided shortly after 10:00 p.m., Tom walked outside to look around. After finding his once-empty bucket full of ten inches of rain, he knew something big was about to happen. Looking across Hart Run, he saw a neighbor. He yelled, "It just rained over ten inches!" And his neighbor

Seybert's Sunoco Garage (*right, background*). *Karen Seybert.*

called back, "I believe it!" Tom told him that it was going to flood and that it would probably come quickly. Standing in the light rain, they talked for less than a minute.

Looking up Hart Run, they saw a three- to four-foot wall of floodwater coming downstream toward them. It was flowing bank full. They started to walk away but quickly began running. The neighbor ran to his house, and Tom ran toward the garage.

Tom's thoughts were immediately of his neighbor across SR 68. Mae was in her eighties and lived alone in an old one-story house. The house and property were prone to nuisance flooding from Sugar Creek. He knew she needed to get out of the house and to higher ground. He was certain that she would be getting water in her house, so he ran across the road and knocked on her door. Mae came slowly. Tom told her that the creek was rising quickly and that she needed to get out. After a moment, she agreed. Tom asked her to get ready while he retrieved his truck.

When he returned, Mae was standing at the door, waiting. Tom helped her into his truck and then closed her house door. Water was already flowing into Mae's home. As Tom began to pull away, Mae asked for her house keys. He had left them in the door lock. Tom could tell by the look on her face how important they were, so he fought his urgency to flee and ran back to get them. By now, the truck was sitting in three inches of water, and it was rising fast.

Tom hoped to go beyond Millionaire Row to a tiny hillside community above Brady's Bend, where he would ask someone to shelter Mae. As he drove, he crossed over Hart Run with no problem. Fifteen yards farther, in front of Brady's Bend Hotel, it appeared that the road was covered with surface runoff. In another fifteen yards, he crossed the bridge at the intersection of Cove Run and Sugar Creek. The water covered the road. He realized that his original idea would not work.

He looked for a place to turn around, aiming to go back to a nearby highpoint—the railroad tracks that crossed Kittanning Hollow Road adjacent to Hart Run. As he slowed his truck, the water started to rise rapidly, from six inches to a foot in a matter of seconds. Chris Henderson's home was on his left, and on his right was the Bartoes's.

He told Mae that they needed to go back. Rather than risk turning around, he decided to drive in reverse. When he did so, he passed a small, two-door Chevy Chevette. The car had just left Brady's Bend Hotel and was flooded and disabled.

Rodney King was in the driver's seat, and a seven-month-pregnant Monica Andreassi was in the passenger's seat. Tom instantly recognized Rodney, who yelled, "Hey, Tom, *stop*! Help us get out of here!" It took Tom a second to realize that Monica was with him. Monica remembers Tom saying, "If you get out now, I will get you, but I can't wait."

What started out as a simple evening to quell Monica's boredom and provide an escape from the unbearable heat in their tiny upstairs apartment quickly turned into an incomprehensible set of circumstances. Even when they were leaving their apartment for Brady's Bend Hotel and Rodney expressed concerns about the weather, Monica said, "Oh, it's rain for God's sake, let's just get out of here!"

A Bronx native, Monica had followed her mother to Brady's Bend after her father died unexpectedly a few years before. She radiates humor and energy, and her lively fast-talking Bronx accent is evident as she describes her experience forty-four years later.

Monica was sitting in a stalled car with doors that wouldn't open and the windows down. With Tom stopped beside them, Rodney climbed out the window and told Monica that she had to get out. Even with Tom screaming, "We need to go now! We need to go! We need to go!" Monica hesitated, saying that she was pregnant and couldn't get out of the car. She remembered being calm but admitted that wasn't typical for her. Rodney was losing patience. He told her to climb over the seat. Monica said, "He was being very forceful with me because Tommy said, 'Come *now* because the water is coming." Monica hesitated again. She protested that she had flip-flops on and that they were dangerous to walk in. Finally, Rodney yelled, "Get in the driver's seat!" Monica admits today that she doesn't know how she fit across the stick shift because of her size in pregnancy, but somehow, she maneuvered into the driver's seat.

As soon as she was in the seat, Rodney reached in and yanked her through the window and stood her straight up. He picked her up under her knees and dropped her on the bed of the truck.

Monica was no longer calm. She had felt the racing water, timber and debris washing by her legs. She had left her flip-flops and purse behind. She was screaming and crying. She was soaking wet. She panicked. She worried that she was losing the baby.

Driving in reverse, within seconds, Tom was up the knoll and on the railroad tracks. He parked his truck. Mae stayed put. Holding onto one another, Rodney and Monica climbed out. The first thing Rodney did was enter the closest home that was out of the path of the water. No one was there; nevertheless, he removed bedding, blankets and a shower curtain to wrap around Monica. Eventually, they walked to higher ground at Daman Industries. Workers found dry work clothes from their storeroom for Monica.

Tom walked back to the garage along the railroad tracks and across a trussell bridge. The lights were still on in the garage, and he could see through the back windows that water was starting to flow onto the garage's concrete floor.

He moved off the railroad tracks and entered through the back door. He stepped into about six inches of water, and it was rising. He decided to raise as many cars as possible. He started with his sister's. Conveniently, there was a floor jack near the rear of the car and a chain-fall pulley directly over its front. He jacked the car up as far as he could with the floor jack and pulleyed the front high enough that it appeared to be dangling from the ceiling. As he turned to raise more cars, he saw his brother Andy wading in the water behind him.

Andy worked at Daman Industries, behind the garage on the high side of the railroad tracks. He worked in the shop beside an open door and had been watching as the creek came up level with the road below. When the water entered the parking lot, he knew something was very wrong. Soon, several inches of water were in the shop, and Daman's shut down. So, Andy walked to his family's garage.

Andy joined Tom, focusing on saving as many cars as they could. They went to the 1970 Plymouth Fury convertible that their brother had purchased a week earlier. They jacked it up with two air jacks. Amazingly, the shop compressor was still working, so they had compressed air for the jacks. They located two more hydraulic lift jacks and went to a customer's car. Then they moved another two floor jacks and elevated a second customer car.

Before they started working, Tom had called his brother John at home to tell him they needed help because "water was coming into the garage." John and his brother Joseph were both at home. In the business's tow truck, they hurried to help. John drove.

After attempting to reach the garage directly from Kittanning Hollow Road, they soon discovered that Hart Run's flooding had submerged the road's last half mile. They were forced to turn back.

They tried two other detours, including one that took them on SR 68 in Kaylor, where they began to "feel buoyancy, and John put it in reverse and quickly found grip and got out of there." Finally, they resorted to driving along a local dirt road that led to the state gamelands, where they took the gameland's grassy hilltop road that runs parallel to Kittanning Hollow Road. They drove until they were above Daman Industries, where they parked the truck and began descending the hillside to their family's business.

At the same time, Andy and Tom were wading in eighteen inches of water, and it was still rising. When they looked around, debris was floating. A few trash cans had been toppled into the floodwaters; oil was on the water surface; and two thirty-five-gallon drums, partially filled with transmission oil, had been tipped and were now floating and leaking. They found the resourceful Lace lying on a workbench, wagging her tail, happy to see them. When they felt they had done all they could, Andy returned to Daman's. Tom planned to follow him outside after he checked the east side of the building, where he waded in two feet of water and noticed that the water level no longer seemed to be rising.

When Tom stepped outside of the garage, he thought he heard screams for help. Atop the hillside, his brothers heard those same screams. Daman's work crew heard them. Rodney heard them, too, and said, 'Then the screaming started. It was terrible. Everybody took off. The screaming was coming from the road just below Seybert's garage." Monica recalled hearing horrible things, "People screaming and animals howling."

The Robinsons and Mary Pistorius

Tom hurried about thirty yards along the railroad track embankment and saw two disabled vehicles along SR 68 in the floodwaters. One was a sedan that had been pushed into the guardrails. It was Mary Pistorius's car. It appeared that the moving water had pushed the car against the highway guardrails and disabled it. Mary's car did not seem to be in danger of moving. The other vehicle was a pickup truck with a cap over the bed. The truck was closer to Sugar Creek with water up to the top of its wheel wells.

Tom recognized the screaming voices. They belonged to Butch Robinson; his wife, Betty Ellen; and their four-year-old daughter, Amy. They were on the roof of the truck cab and cap.

Earlier that evening, Betty Ellen and Mary hosted an in-home party, inviting their friends to view and sample merchandise. The party was at Betty Ellen's home, and Mary was the demonstrator. According to Mary's daughter Cheryl, "The party ended, and the guests left. Mary was visiting with Betty Ellen when Butch came in and said, 'I think we need to get out of here.'"

Before the party, Barry Robinson had chatted with his uncles Butch and Pete, who were standing outside. Barry had recently married, his mobile home placed temporarily behind his dad's home on the Robinson campus. The mobile home was scheduled to be moved to a permanent location the following day. In need of an awning, Barry and his wife planned to shop in a nearby town. When Barry told his uncles of their plans, he asked his uncle Pete if he and his aunt Elinor would care for their nine-month-old son, assuring them that they'd be "back in a few hours." They said, "Sure." Barry and his wife left. Little did they know that was going to be the last time they saw Butch.

Barry later learned that Pete and Butch, along with their friends Carolyn and Butch Yori and their cousins Corky Robinson (chief of the East Brady firemen) and his wife, Gail, were visiting. The women were inside with Betty Ellen and Mary. The men were outside drinking beer and watching the weather. As the party ended, Carolyn and Butch Yori encouraged the group to go to their home, which was purportedly to higher ground, about a mile and a half up SR 68.

Butch had gone to Pete's house and said, "The creek, it's really coming up. We better get the heck out of here." That's when he untied the dogs and went inside to warn Betty Ellen, Amy and Mary that they needed to flee.

Pete and Elinor, with baby in hand, agreed with Butch and Carolyn Yori's plan to go to their home. Before Corky left Butch's home, he called the East Brady Firehall and implored his cousin Paul Robinson, who was working bingo, to not return home. Afterward, Corky and his wife drove toward their home in East Brady. Before they could get into their car, the water reached the top of Corky's cowboy boots.

Butch, Betty Ellen and Amy went in their truck; Mary Pistorius followed in her sedan; Pete, Elinor and the baby were in Pete's car; and Carolyn and Butch Yori brought up the rear in their truck.

"Pete Robinson said when we left our driveway, the water was over our headlights."[32]

In less than a mile, as the caravan approached Seybert's garage, they were in trouble. The rushing water over Pete's headlights caused his car to float and spin around. Continuing with its momentum, he headed back. Instinctively, Carolyn and Butch turned back, too. Butch Robinson's truck continued forward but became disabled near Seybert's garage; behind it was Mary Pistorius's stalled vehicle.

Mary's daughter Cheryl said that Butch helped Betty Ellen and Amy onto the roof of the truck and quickly crossed to help Mary climb out a window and onto the roof of her car before returning to his truck. Mary told Cheryl that she and the Robinsons called back and forth to one another, and then Mary's car was picked up and pushed into the guard rails. She watched debris break through the windshield and back windows of her car, letting water flow freely through.

That's when Tom Seybert heard the Robinsons frightened pleas, "Help us, please help us!" Although water surrounded the truck, it appeared to Tom that the water level was going down. The truck seemed to be staying put. He yelled to Butch, asking if the truck was moving, and Butch yelled back, "No, but if feels a bit wobbly in this flowing water." Tom told them that the water was too high and swift for him to get to them but that it should be dropping soon and that he thought their best bet was to stay where they were to wait for the water to go down enough so they could walk away. Butch agreed, and said he hoped Tom was right.

Tom returned to the garage to look for something, "rope, cable, anything," that he could use to reach the Robinsons. He found nothing. He went back outside a few minutes later and could hear Mary Pistorius wailing. The pickup truck, along with Butch, Betty Ellen and Amy, were gone. Mary's daughter Cheryl said, "My mother saw the truck roll and get swept away with the Robinsons."

Mary Pistorius's experience was recorded in the August 18, 1980, Oil City newspaper *The Derrick.*

> *Mary Pistorius watched in horror as a rampaging creek swept away two of her friends and their young daughter. "I happened to look over where they were," recalled Mrs. Pistorius, who was clinging to her own car as the current of Sugar Creek swirled about her. "Their truck flipped over and they disappeared and I didn't hear them holler anymore....I wish I could have helped them but they couldn't get to my car. The current was so strong it just roared."*
>
> *Mrs. Pistorius had been doing a home goods demonstration at Betty Ellen and Butch's house that night. She was getting ready to leave when Butch persuaded her to stay. "Stay a little bit. It's raining so hard. We'll have something to drink," he said. Robinson went outside to check on his dogs. When he returned his voice showed alarm. "We have to go. We're surrounded by water." As they left the house, the water was already up to their knees. Mrs. Pistorius headed to her car, the Robinsons got in their pickup truck, and they started driving up Route 68 in Brady's Bend. After a distance, Mrs. Pistorius said her car just seemed to stop dead near the Robinson truck.*

> *Butch Robinson got out, water up to his waist, and told Mrs. Pistorius to get out of her car and up onto its roof.... The current was so strong. "We hollered for help and the men at Daman's* [a nearby plant] *heard us calling but said they couldn't get to us. The water kept coming faster and harder. I happened to look over to where they* [the Robinsons] *were. Their truck flipped over and they disappeared and I didn't hear them holler anymore."*[33]

Tom was in disbelief and sick to his stomach. He wondered, "What happened to them? How could the water take them away? They had already survived the deepest water. It was receding." He was dumbfounded; it made no sense.

The Robinsons' calls for help were heard by others on both sides of Sugar Creek. One of Daman's employees wanted to take the company's forklift into the flooding waters to try to reach them. But the other employees talked him out of it, knowing that the forklift would likely stall and may even be washed away.

As my brother Jim struggled to drive from St. Patrick's Church to our kenneled dog, he said that when the high water forced him to turn his car around, he was below Seybert's. The noise of the water was deafening. He thought he heard people yelling but couldn't make sense of what he was hearing. He saw people nearby who he thought were moving toward the sound, trying to help. He couldn't move forward, so he turned back.

David Cassesse, whose family home was just beyond Seybert's garage, was watching the flooding from his front porch with his neighbor. Dave said, "We could hear people yelling and we started to walk up towards the bridge below Seybert's, but the water was rising to our chest, so we turned back to the house."

Crestfallen, Tom returned to the shop. Lace was still on the workbench, so he carried her out the back door and put her down at the top of the railroad embankment. Even unleashed, Lace clung to him as they walked to his truck. He placed her in the cab with Mae and crawled in, too. They watched the water as it carried small trees, shrubs, garbage cans, cars with their lights off, cars with their lights on. Tom said, "All were tossed about as if they were toys. We had no idea if people were in the cars." They watched helplessly as the floodwaters filled the width of the valley. Water was flowing everywhere for as far as they could see in the dark. Tom couldn't stop thinking about Butch Wilson, his wife and his daughter.

The next day, after the sun came up and the water was down, Tom discovered the reason for the movement of the Robinson truck. He walked

The Robinson truck, half a mile from Seybert's Garage. *David Cassesse.*

to the spot where the truck sat and saw evidence that two wheels were on the highway pavement, and two wheels were on the berm. He hadn't realized this the night before. The flooding water had eroded the berm, eventually tilting the truck until it rolled into the creek.

Disbelief

While sheltering at Daman's, Rodney noticed the electric and landline phones were still in operation. Monica called her mother, who lived in a small hillside community. Monica told her, "We lost our car," and her mother, said, "Where did you leave it?" Only a mile away, she could not fathom what was happening in Brady's Bend.

Kelly McNaughton had a similar experience when she called her mother: "After the water receded some, we went to Jackie's dad's house. I think it was about 2:00 a.m., and I finally got a phone line out and called home. My mother answered and I told her, 'It's me. I'm over in Brady's Bend. I was at Tony's bar and this fourteen-foot wall of water came through. You need to call Matt's dad and tell him that Matt's with me and he's OK, and call Alfred

[Debbie's dad] and tell him that Debbie's with me. She's OK.'" Her mother told her that if she was at Tony's bar, she wasn't going to call a single person. It was 2:00 a.m., and the creek in August didn't touch her ankles. If Kelly was drinking, she was to stay put. "Don't drive!" Her mother then hung up.

Kelly got another phone call out at 4:00 a.m. and reached her dad. When she finally saw her mother, she told her, "Next time, I will call Grandma, because she will worry about me. I will skip you."

Kelly said that her sister Patty was on her way home from work when the flood started and "drove home through it. She was right ahead of it. The water was up over her wheels, and she kept moving."

While my brother Jim was on the hillside overlooking our dog's kennel, the lightning lit up the small town below. Disbelief overtook him as he looked down on Upper Brady's Bend; he watched the wooden railroad trestle that sat at the junction of Sugar Creek and Holder Run collapse.

He was shocked. He couldn't believe what he was seeing. The weight of the trestle in the violent waters was moving so fast that it took out everything in its path. With the light from homes and intermittent lightning, he watched the trestle crush five Millionaire Row garages, like dominoes, in one fell swoop.

Eventually, Jim learned that those railroad ties were part of a horror and a salvation in Upper Brady's Bend. Rodney King saw the ties settle against the Pezzuti's store door, protecting a huge display window. Amid the horror, this resting place seemed like a well-deserved miracle for the store owners, who were known as the some of the most pious Catholics in Brady's Bend.

Emma Bedner, the owner of Pezzuti's store, adjacent to Brady's Bend Hotel, said, "It's a miracle that she's still alive and that the sixty-year-old Pezzuti's store continues to serve the residents of the Brady's Bend community." She went to bed early that night,

> *hiding from the sounds of the fierce thunder and the flashes of lightning that preceded the flood. A crashing door on the first floor brought her quickly downstairs, and in the darkness, she remembers almost tripping over a scythe that the waters had lifted out of the cellar. It was the cellar door swept open by the flood waters that roused her from her bed. Then she watched from a side window as the flood rushed toward her store. But miraculously, she believes a heavy railroad trestle, washed down by the flood, wedged against the front of the store diverted the water away from the building.*[34]

Amy Miller also recalled seeing my brother Jim with a small flashlight on the hillside above her aunt's home. Jim had worked his way across the hillside and up Cove Run before he descended. He met Amy's uncle, who suggested they check on older woman who lived in a small trailer next to Cove Run Creek. The woman's daughter-in-law lived in the family home several yards farther away from the creek, against the hillside. As a young, fit twenty-year-old, Jim questioned his ability to make it through the swift waters separating him from the small trailer. He clearly remembers his fear but does not remember how they eventually made it to the trailer. They woke the older woman. Confused, she told them to wait while she retrieved a metal box. They took her and her box to her daughter-in-law's house next door.

In the early hours of the morning, Jim and the rest of my family returned home and went to bed. Not long after, they were awakened by a neighbor yelling from outside, "Jim! Jim! Got your dog! I got your dog!" He had found our pregnant bloodhound a half mile from our home on top of a pile of debris, near St. Patrick's Church. Miraculously, the dog survived by swimming in her kennel until the water was high enough for her to go over the top. She was alive! Did her pregnancy increase her buoyancy? If only she could have told us her story.

A few days later, she delivered eleven puppies inside our home. A few weeks afterward, she died from gastric torsion (bloat). Her puppies were fed and kept clean amid the chaos and filth of cleanup.

MIDDLE BRADY'S BEND

The devastation in Middle Brady's Bend extended from immediately after Seybert's garage to Whiskey Run along Queenstown Road, slightly less than one mile. Sugar Creek crisscrosses SR 68 several times through this area, with the valley alternating between its widest openings and shallower turns.

Cassesses, Coradis and Mellishes

With large brown eyes and a dynamic and engaging energy, Dave Cassesse gave a thoughtful and self-effacing recounting of August 14, 1980. While he admits a modest memory, he offers details of his experience at twenty-four years old that reveal the values of young man with a love of life, family and friendships.

He was a member of The Associates softball team, and his game that night had been canceled due to the rain. Dave recalled, "It was all our buddies, our friends. All our neighbor guys. We weren't real great ballplayers, but we were all great friends." The closeknit group met, after each game, at Brady's Bend Hotel for a hot sausage sandwich and a beer. That night, Dave didn't stay very long. He went home and, without changing from his uniform, settled down on his beanbag to watch a ball game.

Dave lived with his father, Sam, and stepmother, Betty. Their home was three hundred yards below Seybert's garage. The Coradis' house was immediately before the Cassesses'. Besides being neighbors, Sam and Bill Coradi were great friends—so much so that they often consulted each other and then bought identical big-ticket items, like riding tractors and sheds. The Coradis' house was in one of the locations where Sugar Creek crossed underneath SR 68. The creek then ran alongside and behind their home.

The night of the flood, Bill called the Cassesses to ask if they were watching the creek. Betty turned on their backyard flood lights and saw that the water was over the creek bank. It was meandering through their backyard. That had happened before, so it was not alarming.

Bill called back twenty minutes later. He said, "Are you guys watching this? We need to get out of this house. Can we come over there?" The water had filled the Coradis' basement and was rising to their first floor. Water surrounded the Cassesses', yet their slight elevation kept their house dry.

With the help of the Cassesses, the Coradis and their young grandson dodged debris and crossed through the rising waters. Dave recounted an image he will never forget: the Coradis' basement lights were on and submerged, eerily illuminating the water.

As they discussed crossing the highway to scale the adjacent hillside, they realized that they were too late. The water was too high and swift. They remained at the Cassesses' home.

Before long, the water pressed against the Cassesses' garage door, the pressure threatening its collapse. Sam kicked open the front door and did the same with the back door. Now, water was flowing freely through the garage. The house remained dry. The Coradis weren't so lucky.

As the group kept their eyes on the torrent, Bill's shed was ripped from its mooring. Sam confessed to Dave that he hoped their shed would stay put. Within seconds, Bill's shed collided with the Cassesses', and both were carried away.

The highwater mark at 11:00 p.m. in the Cassesse garage. *David Cassesse.*

At that moment, the power line to Sam's shed was disconnected, stopping a clock in the basement at 10:21 p.m. Sam never started that clock again but left it hanging, time stopped, above his workbench for the remainder of his life. Betty, who had retired as an army lieutenant colonel nurse and served in World War II, the Korean War and Vietnam, observed that the creek broke through at 22:00 (10:00 p.m.).

Moving to the front porch, they watched six to eight feet of water race down SR 68. They'd never seen anything like it, nor did they have any idea of what was happening around them. They knew the water had to go somewhere but couldn't comprehend the destruction it was causing or that people's lives would be lost. Innocently, Dave pleaded, "Please stop raining. Please stop." Not long after that, it did stop. A short time later, the water began receding.

Three houses beyond the Cassesses' sat eighty-year-old Ludwig Mellish and his wife, Katherine's, house. Lud and Katherine were renowned for their remarkable vegetable garden.

On higher ground, Cassesse's house remained dry, while the garage was flooded. *David Cassesse.*

> [When Lud] *noticed water entering his basement, he went down to pull electric fuses. "In five seconds, it came from my knees to my waist. I was lucky to get out. I got to the first step and it was up to my neck." Mellish and his wife Katherine went to the first floor where two feet of rampaging water tossed their furniture about. They moved to the second floor. Mellish recalled, "My wife said, 'What are we going to do?' and I said, 'We are going to stay here until it's over or we're going to die.'" Three large walnut trees planted 62 years ago by Mellish disappeared with a torrent. His gardens were covered by at least a foot of rock and mud.*[35]

Magnanis, DeBaccos, Andreassis and Stimacs

The daughter of Thelma and Tony Pezzuti, Marilyn married Tom Magnani. In 1980, Marilyn, Tom and their four young children lived a handful of houses down from the Mellishes'. Directly across from the Magnani house is the DeBaccos', and directly beyond the Magnanis' is the Andreassis' with the Sugar Creek running behind them. The DeBaccos' house was situated on higher ground, nestled against the hillside across SR 68.

Today, Marilyn Magnani's smile and broadmindedness are contagious. She openly shows off her recent tattoo, designed by her granddaughter.

During my younger years when I asked my parents' permission for a tattoo, they said, "They are permanent! Are you sure you'll still want that when you are 70?" Marilyn waited until her seventies to get her first and is delighted.

During our lively conversation, her mothering instincts were on full display. Describing the night of the flood, she reflected on her worries for the safety of her children (the baby and a two-, five- and seven-year-old).

Because of the hard rain, Tom was responding to his mother's call for help as water entered her basement. Tom's mom lived near the Mellishes, across SR 68. Like the DeBaccos', her home was slightly elevated. Nonetheless, she was getting a basement full of water from the hillside runoff. Even though her home was only a few hundred yards away, Tom took one of their cars and parked it against the hillside. No sooner had he arrived than Marilyn called him back, as she watched the water come up their outside steps. Tom left the car at his mother's and ran home.

Marilyn believes that if it weren't for her garage protecting her home from being directly assaulted, her house would have been swept away. She also is grateful that Tom left one car protected against his mother's hillside, because the other floated in their garage. She is even more grateful for the help of Butch Yori, who, with Tom, carried the Magnani children through the swift current across the highway to refuge at the DeBaccos'. Before the end of the night, twenty-eight people were sheltering in one home, that of Florence and Victor DeBacco.

And, yes, it was the same Butch Yori who was following Pete and Elinor Robinson with the baby; Butch, Betty Ellen and Amy Robinson; and Mary Pistorius. When the Yoris and Pete and Elinor turned around, they sought shelter at the DeBaccos'.

Now ninety-three years old, with a sharp memory and a lifetime of knowledge of Brady's Bend, Florence DeBacco believes that God guided survivors to her home that night. She and others considered reaching the safety of the DeBacco house a miracle.

As the flood started, Marilyn was rocking her youngest children, who were upset by the sound of thunder and lightning. She looked out her front window, where she saw Butch Robinson driving by with water surging over the sides and hood of his truck.

She had started watching the creek as she got calls from friends and family urging her to look at the water. That's when she realized that Tom needed to return home. Without him, she wondered how she would get the kids out or whether she should even try. She also realized that the slightly wider valley at her home meant that Butch Robinson was driving toward a narrower valley and higher water.

After turning around near Seybert's garage, Butch and Carolyn Yori stopped immediately beyond the DeBaccos' at St. Patrick's Roman Catholic Church. Carolyn stayed at the church rectory while Butch helped the Magnanis. Marilyn remembers that Tom and Butch took the babies first and came back for the two oldest children—daughters. One daughter froze. Marilyn had never experienced anything like it. Her daughter was frozen solid. Immovable. Marilyn slapped her to snap her out of it. Then one of the men picked up the girl and carried her to safety.

Marilyn was the last to cross. She said it felt like the water was hitting her chest. Tom told her not to lift her legs but to shuffle. So, she shuffled the entire way with diapers and baby bottles in her hands. They stayed at the DeBaccos' until after 1:00 a.m.

Before their refugees arrived, the DeBaccos were attending to their own storm troubles. The two youngest of their six children were at home: ten-year-old Linda and fourteen-year-old Eddie. Florence remarked that the carefree nature of the evening was no indication of what was to come a few hours later. Linda had been fishing alone along Sugar Creek, caught a little fish and brought it home. They took a picture. Eddie played football for East Brady High School. They had their last practice and then the annual cookout before the season started.

Late in the evening, Florence was busy in the kitchen while her husband, Victor, napped on the couch before his overnight shift at a local refinery. Linda worriedly came to her mother and said, "Mom, the water's coming across the road real bad." After looking out the window, Florence calmly said, "It's just raining hard, Linda." A couple minutes later, Linda woke her father, "Dad. Dad. There's a lot of water coming across the road. What's wrong?" Victor was angry that he had been awakened before he needed to leave for work.

Shortly afterward, Linda went to the bathroom. When Victor and Florence heard her screaming, they went to look. She was on the toilet with a tree limb protruding through the window. The hillside behind the DeBaccos' had become like quicksand; it was raining so hard that trees were being uprooted and falling.

Then the phone rang. It was Florence's sister Jenny Stimac, who lived less than a quarter mile down SR 68. She asked Florence if they were getting any water in their basement. Looking down at the basement steps, Florence saw the water was up two steps. As they continued talking, Jenny told Florence that a boat was floating by her window and that their door had broken loose.

Everything began happening quickly. Someone knocked. Elinor and Pete Robinson with the baby were there. They asked if they could come in and park their car at the DeBaccos' house. They said, "Sure." As the Robinsons entered the house, their car was lifted from the driveway and carried off. Victor and Eddie ran to the basement, exited and tied their car down. Within minutes, the water wrenched their car away, too.

Marilyn and Tom arrived with their four kids; Tom had one on each arm. As the family entered, the water became more treacherous; it was a miracle they hadn't been swept away. Butch Yori followed behind.

Then the DeBaccos' neighbors Roland and his wife, with their home against the same hillside, called and asked if they could come over with their three sons. Florence said yes and said it was safest to enter through the back door. Eddie was waiting for them. Roland and his three sons came into the house. Roland said, "My wife needs help." The ground behind the home was like quicksand, and Roland's wife was stuck. Victor and Roland pulled her out. Florence gave Roland's mud-covered wife some of Victor's clothes to change into.

Before the night was over, the DeBaccos would have twenty-eight people in their home, four of whom were babies. Florence used tea towels for diapers and diaper pins leftover from her own six kids. Then she, Eddie and Linda emptied the refrigerator and the cupboards. Crackers, cereal, whatever was there. Everyone ate. They brought out games for the kids. Putting aside what was happening outside, Florence was thankful to be able to provide her visitors with a place of safety and fellowship.

At the light of day, someone arrived at the DeBaccos' door. They were counting people. They wanted to know who was in their home. They were looking for the Robinsons.

Across the road from the DeBaccos' home was Silvio "Scabby" and Shirley Andreassi's home. Today, Scabby and Shirley are rightfully proud of the accomplishments of their seven adult children (four boys and three girls who were between the ages of five and nineteen at the time of the flood).

A week before the flood, Scabby had returned from a trip to Italy, and Shirley was relieved not to be home alone. Their oldest son was away, visiting a friend. Two of their children had returned from band practice earlier that evening. By the time they arrived home, the rain had started. When the flooding began, they called the DeBaccos but concluded that the water was too high to cross.

They knew they were in trouble as water rushed down the highway. They watched the Magnani family cross to the DeBaccos' house. Scabby exclaimed, "Oh my God, they're going to be swept away!" The increasing ferocity and depth of the growing river around their home made them realize how lucky the Magnanis were.

The Andreassis' house now sat in the middle of a river. Within minutes, the water was in their living room, above their window, three and then four feet above the first floor. Everything was being battered by water and debris. Above the noise, they heard creaking. The force of the water was pulling the wrought-iron railing off their back porch. Their detached wooden garage and two cars were carried away with a mower and a lifetime supply of tools and hardware.

Scabby sent Shirley and the children upstairs and told them to stay in a bedroom, not to look outside. He worried that they would see the wreckage striking the house—or worse yet, that the house would break open.

The Andreassi house with its first-floor windows open. *David Cassesse.*

Scabby opened the first-floor windows and doors to let the water flow through. Their floating refrigerator hit him in the back, so he shoved it out the door and onto the front porch.

It wasn't until the water receded that the Andreassi family crossed the road to the DeBaccos'. Holding onto each other, their feet sinking into the mud with each step, they crossed the uneven ground.

While some homes had water only in their basements, the Andreassi home suffered terribly; they had a watermark four feet on the wall of their first floor. Like Marilyn Magnani, Scabby said that they had seen Butch Robinson's family drive by their home. When the water receded, the Robinson truck was just beyond their backyard.

While the DeBaccos sheltered those fleeing to safety, farther down SR 68, Florence's sister Jenny and her husband, Joe, were grappling with how to get their son Carl, who was paralyzed from the neck down, to their second floor. Jenny and Joe Stimac had six children, four boys and two girls. The boys were powerful football players. Two years before the flood, sixteen-year-old Carl, a superior athlete, was injured during a high school football game. After months of hospital stays and rehabilitation, Carl returned home. His bed was placed in the first-floor dining room. He required twenty-four-hour care and a respirator to breathe.

Jenny told Florence that as the water began to flood their kitchen, they knew that they had to move Carl upstairs. Florence didn't recall who was

Stimac's adaptive van, a half mile from their home. *John M. Olszak.*

able to get Carl up the steps with its switchback in the middle. She only knew it was a daunting task.

Once upstairs, they used a car battery to power Carl's respirator. In the early morning hours, while it was still dark, Joe Curran, whose interview is highlighted in the next section, and his neighbor investigated damage along SR 68. As they walked by the Stimacs' house, Joe Stimac called out from his porch, "Can you fellas give us a hand bringing Carl down from the upstairs." By then, the car battery was nearly depleted. Joe Stimac instructed the four men to create a stretcher with their arms.

Joe Curran said that they carried Carl down the steps, with Carl's dad carrying the battery. At the bottom of the steps, Joe was soaked from head to toe with sweat and wondered how on earth they gotten Carl upstairs. Later that day, Carl was transported to a local medical center for care while his family addressed the damage to their home and intermittent access to electrical power.

> *The Joe and Jenny Stimac family from Brady's Bend had its two-week old garage worth $6,000 severely damaged, and lost the van used to transport their son Carl, the East Brady High School football player who was paralyzed from the neck down in a football accident in October 1978. The specially-designed van was purchased with contributions from the community and valued at about $15,000. "We lost everything in our cellar…and we might have lost Carl too if we hadn't gotten him upstairs. The water came up on the front porch. We didn't take any chances. We picked him up and carried him upstairs. I really feel bad for Carl, because now we can't take him anywhere," said Mrs. Stimac. During the last football season, Carl could be seen taking in East Brady High football games from his van parked beyond the end zone. Now he can't go.*[36]

Two months after the flood, on October 21, 1980, Carl died, exactly two years to the day of his accident. Throughout the entire ordeal, from Carl's accident and the flood, the trials of Carl and his family were handled with grace and determination. Jenny told Florence that the night before Carl died, he asked his mother to keep his siblings quiet while they got ready for school because he was tired and wanted to sleep in.

Two more of Florence's sisters lived with their mother across from the Stimacs' home on SR 68. The Galassi home was on the hillside above the highway, where it, too, became a refuge for a family, the Dunmyres.

Eighty-year-old Julia Dunmyre lived in a trailer behind her son and daughter-in-law's home. Her son was not home that evening, so as the water rose, her daughter-in-law took her young daughter and Julia across the road and climbed the driveway to the Galassi house. No sooner had they arrived than Julia's trailer washed away. Years later, Angie Galassi attended Julia's son's funeral and met the adult child who'd come to her house that night. That child gave her a big hug and said, "Angie, I'll never forget the night of the flood. You put me in bed, and you gave me that little teddy bear that I still have today. Thank you."

Downings, Currans and Ions

Eighty-seven-year-old Catherine "Cathy" Downing had been married to Wilson for twenty-one years. Cathy said, "Wilson gave me my diamond on Valentine's Day during my senior year in high school. We married after his military service ended. I still wear that diamond ring today."

Wilson died in 2022 after sixty-three years of marriage. Their two sons, Joe and John, were teenagers in 1980. The night of the flood, Wilson was working strike duty in West Virginia. Neither he nor Cathy realized the severity of the storm—Wilson because of his distance from home and Cathy because their well-insulated house kept the sound at bay. It wasn't until a next-door neighbor knocked at her door and asked if she was all right that she realized something was wrong. Floodwater surrounded her house.

Cathy's two sons raced upstairs to a window. They saw Julia Dunmyre's trailer float between two houses, hit a building and disintegrate. Everything that was inside the trailer created a stew of wreckage in the churning water. More debris swept by. The oldest son asked about their car—should they take it out of the garage? His mother thought it was safer for them to stay in the house.

Like some others, the Downings' electricity and phone service was never interrupted that night. So, Cathy called her husband. Wilson was immediately released from work and started the hours' drive home.

Similar to others who were trying to reach Brady's Bend, Wilson, when he arrived at Kepples Corner (the origin of Sugar Creek Watershed), was detoured. He was also prevented from going beyond the alternative route, the entrance to Kittanning Hollow Road. He waited at Sugar Creek Firehall, where he learned that heavy equipment would arrive in the morning. Anxious to reach his family, when the equipment arrived,

Wilson was there and hitched a ride for the three-and-a-half-mile drive into Brady's Bend. From there, the destroyed roadways left him no choice but to walk the remaining mile home. He met others along the way; one of whom assured him that his family was safe. Given the images he was seeing, he was overwhelmed with relief.

Beyond the Downings' and on the opposite side of the road sat the home of Wade Ion. Born and raised in Brady's Bend, he has lived in his current home since 1970, shortly after he married Melissa. Luckily, his home sits on a hillside about sixty feet above SR 68. A meat manager at the local Shop 'n Save, Wade was known for his welcoming smile and easygoing nature. In 1980, Wade and Melissa's children were eight and six.

On August 14, Wade and Melissa were cheerfully purchasing new furniture for their TV room. When they arrived home, furniture in tow, it was raining lightly. Melissa's father helped them unload. As the rain picked up, her father left for his home. After arranging their furniture, they sat down to admire their new purchase. Then the power went out. Wade said, "We sat there for a little bit. It must have been around 9:00 p.m., and we decided, let's just go to bed." The children were already in bed. Wade and Melissa could hear the rain but didn't think anything of it. Between 10:00 and 11:00 p.m., somebody banged on the front door, yelling, "Hey, Wade! Hey, Wade!"

Neighbor Mike DiPento and his nephew, his nephew's wife and their three crying children were at the door. Mike asked to come in, telling Wade that his house was gone. His car was gone. His garage was gone. Like many who were unaware of what was happening, Wade innocently asked, "Gone where?"

After they were invited in, Mike and his nephew and his family sat in the kitchen and described their harrowing experience. While trying to settle the crying children, Melissa suggested Wade go to the basement to get a couple liters of soda pop. Wade opened his basement door to see two feet of water below. While their home was elevated from direct flooding, the downhill runoff had filed his basement, as it was doing to many others.

Mike and Wade went outside and walked along the hillside parallel to SR 68. Wade said that it sounded like Niagara Falls. They watched the water roll through the Andreassis' home, through one side and out the other, and on through Saint Patrick's Church. Like many others, Wade described seeing a wild river instead of the creek, roadway and valley. It was incomprehensible.

Wade doesn't remember what time his visitors left, but around 4:00 a.m. his boss, the owner of Shop 'n Save grocery store in East Brady, called and asked if he could come to work. The store was full of water. Many of the displays had collapsed. His boss needed help cleaning. While Wade's home was only one and a half miles from the store, Wade told him that he couldn't get there. Like many others who were not in the direct path of Brady's Bend's flooding, his boss was puzzled. He asked, "What do you mean you can't get here?" Wade told him that the highway was gone, washed out. He promised that once daylight came, he would walk the hillsides to get to the store.

Another one hundred yards beyond the Ion home sat the home of Joe and Elaine Curran and their three-year-old daughter. Joe and Elaine's home sits slightly off SR 68 on Saint Mary's Cemetery Road. It overlooks SR 68, elevated about forty feet above the roadway. At the time of the flood, Elaine was five months pregnant with their second child.

Before my first discussion with Joe, I had been told that he had an amazing memory and was relied on as the resident historian with an exceptional knowledge of local railroad history. Both his father and father-in-law had careers with the railroad, so Joe's appreciation for all things railroad began at an early age.

During several conversations with Joe, I came to respect and envy the peculiarity of his memory. His wife, Elaine, said that at Joe's fiftieth high school class reunion, he was the emcee. He greeted the group by asking his classmates if they remembered what they were wearing on the first day of seventh grade. He then went on to answer his question for each of them.

When I asked Joe to share his memories of the flood, he provided remarkable details for a twenty-four-hour period, starting on August 14, 1980, at 4:45 a.m., when he got up for work, to the early morning hours of August 15, 1980.

In 1980, Joe worked as a welder repairman for Black Fox Mining at a site about fourteen miles from his home. In Joe's words, Black Fox was "strip mining coal and I was repairing the 475 Michigan that broke the mounting brackets out of the mainframe. I was putting them back in that day."

He recalled the intensity of the humidity as he stepped outside to leave for work. The sky was full of clouds. It looked like the rain would fall out of them at any instant, "like you could reach up and touch them."

When Joe arrived at his job site, he stopped at an old bus where supplies were stored. The superintendent was signing the daily log, indicating he had inspected the mining job. He lightheartedly asked Joe, "What do you want?" Joe responded, "I don't want it to rain today." The superintendent folded his hands and bowed his head in prayer, saying, "Dear Lord, don't let it rain on my big welder today [Joe is a six-foot-one-inch-tall, big-framed man] so he can fix my machine."

Joe recalled working the entire day in intense humidity. At 4:30 p.m., quitting time, he asked a couple of the workers on the afternoon shift for directions to Thompson's Market. His parents had seen Thompson's advertisement for peaches in the local newspaper. So, Joe detoured from his usual route home. After buying a bushel of peaches, he continued home. Halfway through his drive, shortly after 5:00 p.m., the rain "let loose a tremendous rain, torrential downpour." As he pulled onto Route 268, there was only one lane for travel. It had rained so much, each side of the road looked like a creek. Before he proceeded, he paused to let the one-lane traffic go. When he looked in his rearview mirror, he saw the superintendent. He was on his way home. Joe jumped out of his truck, ran back and handed him six peaches.

Joe arrived home and delivered the peaches to his parents, who lived just below his house along SR 68. His parents were getting ready for a holy day mass at St. Patrick's Church. Joe asked his dad, Carl, a fellow welder, "Do you want to go with me and weld tomorrow?" Carl said, "I'm not going in the rain." So, Joe went home for supper. The rain had stopped, but it looked like more would come. By the time Joe's parents left for evening mass, it was raining again.

Shortly before 8:00 p.m., Joe had his welding gear loaded on his truck for the next day. It had stopped raining again, and the sky turned the most beautiful pink that Joe had ever seen. Encouraged that it wouldn't rain Friday, Joe returned to again ask his dad, "You want to go? It's going to be nice tomorrow. Look at that sky." Carl said, "Well, I don't have the truck loaded." Joe offered to load Carl's truck and then did just that. He returned home close to 9:00 p.m., got a shower and read the paper. Then it started to rain again.

Joe, like many others, confessed that he didn't think too much about the rain and went to bed. He had just gotten into bed when his wife came in and said, "There's water running in the basement." He hurried to the basement. The water inside was three feet deep against the storm door. Little waterfalls were coming inside. He thought the drain was plugged, so he opened the door to let the water out. It didn't take him long to realize the problem wasn't the drain, it was the rain.

Joe swept up the best he could. Elaine returned a few minutes later to tell Joe that his dad was coming up the hill. Joe ran upstairs to his porch to see his dad walking up the gravel road to their house with his four-buckle Arctics. This is when he noticed the depth of the runoff on his dad's boots.

At this point, in Middle Brady's Bend, the roaring river was growing. Five of Sugar Creek's six tributaries had dumped into the creek. All the hillsides'

The remains of Butch Robinson's modular home with its frame wrapped around a tree. *Tim Patsy.*

runoff from the ridges, crags and cliffs had ballooned those tributaries. The tributaries, in turn, assaulted the creek to a point that it no longer existed. It was a river, and everything it had collected was transformed into a violent assault on the entire valley floor; even the valley's width was no match for what had been unleashed.

Fifty yards beyond Carl's home was the Robinson campus. Carl told Joe that he watched Butch Robinson's double-wide modular home get picked up by the water, cross the road, float through the elementary school yard, hit a tree and "disintegrate into a million pieces." At the time, neither Joe nor Carl knew if the Robinsons were home. They were not, although leaving home hadn't spared them their fate.

Barry Robinson's mobile home did the same. Lifted by the water, it washed across the road to the elementary school and disintegrated. A twisted pretzel frame remained.

A neighbor who lived in the house beside Wade Ion drove his truck down Cemetery Road, determined to assist his sister, who lived close to the creek. He had a four-wheel-drive, three-quarter-ton pickup. He saw Joe Curran and his father and stopped, declaring, "I'm going to try to get my sister out of the house. I have ropes and stuff." Joe told him that he wouldn't make

The remains of Barry Robinson's mobile home. *Tim Patsy.*

it. The water covered the road. The neighbor continued down the hill. The water was so high that his truck floated to the bottom of the gravel road. He lost control and sank. Fortunately, his truck went no farther.

Joe and his father returned to their homes. Joe's phone rang, and it was his cousin who lived near the DeBaccos. She asked Joe if she should go to St. Patrick's Church, thinking if anything went wrong, it was best to go to the church to pray. Joe told her that whatever she did, "Do not go to the church!" It was lower than her house. If the water came to her front door, she was to go out the back door and up the hill.

Joe decided to get dressed. He drove his heavy welding truck partway down the hill, parked, turned on his lights and watched three to four feet of water roll by on SR 68 as he wondered, "What in the world is going to happen?" And just that quickly, the rain stopped, and the water began to recede. Within a short time, it had gone from feet to inches on the road.

While Joe sat there, another truck came from the direction of East Brady. The driver rolled down his window, and Joe warned him to get off the road, as he was likely to get stuck. The driver reassured him and turned around to drive to Queenstown Road. Joe learned later that the driver helped three women who were trapped in their car.

Joe left his truck and walked to his parents' home. His mother asked them to cross the road to check on her sister. They were certain his aunt's living room was full of water. Her front porch had been washed away, so Joe and Carl entered through the back. They found her sound asleep. Waking, she said, "What the hell are you two doing here?" When they told her that there was a flood and that houses had washed away, like so many others, she was in disbelief. It made no sense. Although her front porch was gone and her basement was full of water, she didn't have a drop of water on her first floor. They suggested she go back to sleep; they would return in the morning. Before returning home, they disconnected the power from the house.

At home, Joe met his neighbor, and they began investigating along SR 68, eventually assisting Joe Stimac in carrying Carl downstairs. After Joe and his neighbor left the Stimacs' home, they continued along SR 68 toward St. Patrick's Church. Cautiously, before each step, Joe used a stick to check beneath the water to determine if his footing was secure. When they reached the church, they saw a travel trailer wedged against a bridge. Joe dreaded looking inside but did so and was relieved to not find anyone. With nothing more to do to help, they turned back and went home.

Joe went through his basement, kicked off his wet boots and changed his wet jeans to a pair of shorts. He went upstairs, sat in his recliner and didn't

The travel trailer that Joe Curran investigated, with Victor DeBacco Sr.'s car resting against the back. *Tim Patsy.*

remember anything until the phone rang at 5:00 a.m. It was a neighbor who lived across SR 68, near the creek. She wasn't home that evening and wanted to know if her house was still there. Joe told her that from what he saw that night, it was. He immediately fell back asleep; the next thing he knew, it was 7:30 a.m., and Elaine was waking him so he could begin surveying how bad things really were.

Robinsons and Heginbotham

Now in his sixties, Barry Robinson remains a handsome and fit man. Since the flood, his uncles and his parents have passed. He is one of the last of his family members who experienced the flood. With a gracious and inviting demeanor, he welcomed me into his home to talk about his and his family's traumatic experiences on August 14, 1980.

In 1980, Barry Robinson was eighteen years old. He was married to Lesa, and they had nine-month-old Dustin. In Upper Brady's Bend, his uncle Butch, aunt Betty Ellen and cousin Amy were lost in the creek near Seybert's garage. His uncle Pete and aunt Elinor were turned around by the water and found shelter with Victor and Florence DeBacco. Barry's dad, Paul, and mom, Delores, were volunteering at the East Brady Firehall for Thursday night bingo. The only ones at home in the Robinson encampment were Betty Ellen's parents. The Liases were caring for Butch and Betty Ellen's sixteen-year-old son, Tom "T-Turtle" Robinson.

Barry recalls coming home from work in Butler in the late afternoon on August 14. It was raining, which caused him to lament about the amount of rain they had received over the past few weeks. Later that evening, after his backyard conversation with his uncles Pete and Butch, Barry, with Lesa, left baby Dustin in good hands while they went to look at awnings for their trailer. Their trailer was still on wheels, and they had plans to move it the next day to their new property.

While they were leaving the awning shop, it started raining hard. The most direct route from the shop to Brady's Bend is a series of backroads through rural woods and farmland. That's the route Barry and Lesa took when it began raining so hard they could barely see.

Approaching a small depression on the roadway, it looked like a creek was coming down the road. As they tried to drive through, their car stalled. The water was over their headlights. The water's pressure prevented the doors from opening, so Barry and Lesa crawled out the windows. In the darkness and pouring rain, they hung onto the car and then worked their way up the nearby bank.

They were walking in pitch dark in "the hardest rain" Barry had ever experienced. They could barely see each other, yet they continued to walk along the bank beside the roadway. As a driving couple approached, Lesa started screaming. They heard her and stopped. The water reached the vehicle's doors. The driver opened his doors and invited the water-soaked pair to climb in. Barry gave Lesa a quick boost. The man grabbed her and pulled her in. Barry followed. The current knocked him off his feet and pulled him under. Instantly, he grabbed the bottom of the car door. The man grasped his hand.

As Barry reflected on this memory, he said rarely talks about his close call with death because he realizes how lucky he is to be alive when his uncle and family are not.

The couple with Barry and Lesa explored various backroads looking for safe passage. All the roads were closed or cut off by water. They then spotted a residence with a porch light on—that of the Elliots. They knocked at the door and were invited in, sopping wet and covered with mud. Barry and Lesa urgently wanted to call home to check on the safety of their family and to let them know they were safe. The Eliotts' phone wasn't working. Instead, they had a CB radio and were listening to people sharing information about "a major flood in Brady's Bend. A flood with missing people." They heard the Robinson name.

Barry and Lesa's alarm and terror increased. The reports didn't say which Robinsons were missing. Pete's name was mentioned. They knew that nine-month-old Dustin was with Pete and Elinor. Barry said, "We stayed at the Elliots' house all night. It was a terrible night. We kept hearing that there were some Robinsons missing. We heard firefighters talking. We didn't know if our son was safe."

The Elliots' CB finally heard talk from the East Brady Firehall. They learned that Barry's mom and dad were still there but didn't know the fate of the other Robinsons. They held on for a dread-filled night. Some Robinsons were missing. Did that include their son?

The next morning, the Elliots drove Barry and Lesa to Brady's Bend. Washed-out roadways slowed their travel. The Elliots' Jeep worked its way around an obstacle course of debris.

When emergency personnel who were controlling entry into Brady's Bend discovered who the Robinsons were, they let them through. They arrived home to see that Butch and Betty Ellen's home was gone. Theirs was gone.

Brady's Bend Elementary School (*left, background*), August 15, 1980. *David Cassesse.*

But Pete, Elinor and Dustin were there. Processing the destruction, Barry thought, "What the heck happened here?" It's then that he discovered that Butch, Betty Ellen and Amy were the missing Robinsons—but not because their house had been washed away.

Barry also discovered that the Liases, with T-Turtle, had tried to escape in their truck. They made it a few yards before they were stranded on a small patch of higher ground. There, they sat all night surrounded by a torrent. Barry said, "I can't imagine how afraid they were, sitting there all night in that flood. I don't know if they could see things going by. T-Turtle sat in that truck while his mom, dad and little sister didn't survive."

Across the road from the Robinsons sat Brady's Bend Elementary School. Robert Heginbotham was a custodian who was preparing the school for its reopening in a few weeks. He was working when the flood peaked.

> *"I prayed to God quite a bit. I heard this place cracking all over," said Robert Heginbotham, 57, custodian at the elementary school in Brady's Bend in Armstrong County. "The water came up suddenly. It was running really swift. The water was up about two or three feet against the doors on the outside of the school," he said. "I tried to get out and couldn't get the doors open, so I had to stay in. Next thing I see is parts of buildings and automobiles floating by."*[37]

LOWER BRADY'S BEND

Less than a mile long, Lower Brady's Bend begins at Queenstown Road, where the final tributary, Whiskey Run, enters Sugar Creek. At the end of Lower Brady's Bend, Sugar Creek empties into the Allegheny River. While Middle Brady's Bend has a wider valley, this section is the narrowest. It has fewer residences. The hillsides are steeper, with cliffs hugging the roadway, leaving little room for homes. This narrow valley is a snaking trail of switchback turns, with the creek crossing underneath the roadway six times. At its final turn, Sugar Creek becomes a horseshoe before it meets the river. In the center of that horseshoe sit residences and camps.

That night, Lower Brady's Bend was the narrowing neck of a funnel. Entering this funnel, the flood's wreckage increased its speed, force and depth.

Queenstown Road and Whiskey Run

According to newspaper reports and an interview with former East Brady Fireman Jim Curran, three East Brady women had been to a social group meeting that night and later became stranded on Queenstown Road. Hillside runoff, combined with Whiskey Run's overflow, pushed their car to the side of the road, where it sat perilously on a washed-out berm near a bridge. According to Jim, "They sat in the car all night and prayed. They could easily have been flipped upside down from the force of the water. Instead, they listened as water and rocks assaulted their car."

Martin's Texaco

Martin's Texaco sat at the bottom of Queenstown Road. Jim Martin, named after his father, Jim, was sixteen years old at the time of the flood. The oldest of four children and the only boy, Jim is now a chemical engineer working in process safety management. He lives south of Mobile, Alabama, along the Gulf of Mexico and is a true flood veteran; Brady's Bend was his first, with Hurricane Harvey bringing back many memories.

Jim's grandfather was the original owner of Martin's Texaco. By 1980, Jim's father and his mother had taken over this family business located on the bottom floor of Jim's grandfather's house. His grandfather lived on the top floor. In Jim's words, "By then, Grandpa was pretty much confined to bed or his wheelchair because he had lost his legs due to diabetes, but with someone at the store seven days a week, he was able to stay at the house."

Besides being a spot where you could fill up your gas tank, the Texaco was a wonderful place to buy sandwich meats and other staples, as well as the *Sunday Pittsburgh Press*. The Martins were a family with a generous spirit. They had no credit card machine but kept a running tab (that was sometimes forgiven) for customers who were unable to pay.

At Christmastime, Jim's mother made nut rolls, and his dad had a bottle of whiskey handy to celebrate the season. Martin's Texaco was the kind of place where people found an excuse to stop no matter the time of year. It was a place to fill your tank, get staples to pack your lunch or share news—and where children could get a free piece of penny candy.

Jim's family lived in East Brady, and he had just finished his last day of high school football practice. He was home that evening when the storm started. His father called for him, "We gotta go! The creek flooded, and we need to help your grandpa." They jumped in their car and drove the mile to the Texaco.

Martin's Texaco, August 15, 1980. *David Cassesse.*

Forty-four years later, Jim still reflects in amazement, "We got to the gas station and went through the store entrance and ran up the stairs. We said hello to Grandpa. When I opened the upstairs front door and looked out, the water that was puddles when we arrived was halfway up our four-foot retaining wall. It came up that fast and continued to rise. Had we been driving a few minutes later, we would have been swept away and drowned in the river." Jim and his dad remained trapped with his grandpa that night.

Davis Palmer and the Ritcheys

> *Mrs. Edward (Evelyn) Ritchie of Petrolia and her mother-in-law, Mrs. Roy Ritchey of Petrolia were on their way home from a bingo game in East Brady when their car became stalled on Route 68. As the water rose swiftly, the two women got onto the roof of their vehicle and clung for their lives.*[38]

One of Brady's Bend's heroes received nationwide recognition and was presented with the prestigious Carnegie Hero Medal, which is given to persons who've performed outstanding acts of bravery. Davis Alexander Palmer saved the lives of two women, Myrtle and Evelyn Ritchey.

Davis was sixty-three at the time of the flood. According to his daughter Jeanie Bergman and grandson John Slick, Davis's acts of heroism reflected his innate determination. Known throughout the community for his kindness and warmth, Davis was a favorite among all, particularly children.

Jeanie and her son John shine when telling the story of the man who meant so much to them and whose character was evident in every aspect of his life. In two other incidents, Davis saved people from drowning and a young boy from a fire. As a young man, he assisted a young woman with her child at a local swimming site, and in another incident, he ran into a burning building to rescue a young boy. While in the U.S. Army and stationed in Bizerte, Africa, his fellow soldiers were swimming in the Mediterranean when they were caught in riptides. Davis helped nine of those men to safety.

"He has that spirit in him," Jeanie said, "where you don't stand back, you act."

On August 14, Evelyn Ritchey and her daughter-in-law Myrtle were on their way home from East Brady Firehall's Thursday night bingo. Davis was home alone with his five-year-old poodle, Buster. His wife, Jean, and her friends had gone to the Dayton County Fair. Davis, who was very

An oil well that exploded across from Davis Palmer's home. *Tim Patsy.*

hard of hearing and a sound sleeper, was in bed when Buster sounded the alarm. Barking nonstop and running from window to window, Buster finally woke Davis.

Roused, Davis looked out the window, but it was too dark to see anything. He went outside. He thought he heard screaming above the noise of the torrential rain, roaring water and thunder. At that moment, a gas well across the road exploded. Davis later said, "I never heard or saw anything like that except when I was in World War II. The flames were so high and the floodwaters washing over the well made the flames look as if they were moving downstream."

The light from that explosion helped Davis see the women on their car, where the flooding waters had pushed them against the side of the road. They later told him that when a tree hit their windshield, they decided to get out. The high water was causing their car to float. Myrtle helped her mother-in-law out the window and onto the car's roof before she climbed there herself. They were terrified, as the rising waters continued to move their car.

The Palmer home sits about thirty feet above SR 68. When Davis went outside, the bottom of the driveway and lower yard looked like a lake. He drove his car as close to the water as possible to examine the women's predicament. He gauged the water to be over his head and realized the intense current made it impossible for him to reach Evelyn and Myrtle directly.

The Palmers were avid boaters who had a recent family reunion, so their boat was on a trailer in their backyard. Davis returned to the boat, where he retrieved a yellow ski rope, a tire innertube and two life vests.

Returning down the hill, he waded to the edge of the rushing water and tied his rope to a tree. The fire from the oil well had burned out, making it more difficult for him to see—except during periodic lightning. Davis tied the inner tube and a life vest to his rope and threw it twelve to fifteen feet across the debris-filled water to the women.

Eventually, one of the women caught it. They decided that Evelyn, the older of the two, would go first. She put on a life vest and the innertube tied to the rope. It took quite some time for Davis to coax the terrified Evelyn off the car. When she finally dismounted, she hit the water and went under. Davis dove in, fighting through the debris and current to swim to the end of the rope and pull her up. Drained, they stood in the water to catch their breath and regain their strength.

Battling the distance to the tree was grueling. The debris and rushing water turned every step into a contest of man against water and debris.

Exhausted, Davis returned for Myrtle. Although the water was no longer rising, the second rescue was as daunting as the first. The innertube was gone. He threw the rope and life vest to Myrtle. She caught the vest and put it on and dismounted from the car roof into the water.

Davis joined her at the end of the rope. Dodging obstacles and moving deliberately, they wrestled their way tree by tree. Only later did Davis confess his doubts about their ability to hold on as they endured the exhausting effort to advance. Beyond overcoming shear exhaustion, they persisted in battling debris.

The entire ordeal took more than three hours. All were depleted, cut and bruised. They rested at the bottom of the yard before Davis took the women to his home. There, they spent the remainder of the night astonished that they were still alive. The flood had wiped out the Palmers' phone service, so they waited until morning for assistance. The women then went to the hospital so Evelyn could be examined for her heart condition.

While Davis was saving the Ritcheys, his wife, Jean's, car was stuck in the Dayton Fair visitor parking field. Rain and mud were up to the cars' hubcaps. One by one, each car needed to be pulled out to the paved road. After several hours, Jean and her friends began their journey home. They

Left to right: Patrice King Brown from KDKA Pittsburgh 2Day, Myrtle Ritchey, Evelyn Ritchey and Davis Palmer. *Jeanie Bergman.*

were stopped at Sugar Creek Firehall and prevented from proceeding into Brady's Bend. That's where Jean and her friends met Sam Tascarella, who had also been rerouted on his way home from work.

Later, Sam told his daughter Kelly McNaughton that he and Jean began talking, wondering about what was going on. Jean said, "Oh, you know Davis. He's so deaf that he's probably sitting in his chair, sleeping through all this." Little did she know that he was risking his life to save the Ritcheys.

When Sam finally talked to Kelly, he told her that he'd heard over the fire station radio that some young woman had broken three fingers in the door frame at Brady's Bend Hotel. He asked Jean, "Who the hell would be stupid enough to stick their fingers in a door?" When Kelly told him that it was her, he said, "For God's sake, Kelly, if I'd have known you were there, I would have gone ahead and told everyone at the fire station that I know who that has to be."

Davis did sleep, but only through the day after the Ritcheys left. When he awoke later that afternoon, he, too, went to the hospital. His prior open-heart surgery and chest pains worried his family, so he went to be examined. Luckily, all that was found was an exhausted and badly bruised man.

Above: Davis Palmer and Buster at their Brady's Bend home, 1981. *Janice Hamburg.*

Next page: Davis Palmer and Buster's hero medals, 1981. *Jeanie Bergman.*

Davis himself attributes Buster with making the Ritchey women's survival possible. "Buster heard the screams of the terrified women and barked until his master was awakened to the disastrous happening outside of his house."[39]

For those not familiar with the Carnegie Hero Fund Commission, the organization "recognizes outstanding acts of selfless heroism performed in the United States and Canada. The Carnegie Medal is awarded to one who, at the risk of his own life, saves or attempts to save the life of a fellow man."[40] Davis received his medal on March 5, 1981. Shortly afterward, his daughter Jeanie wrote a letter to Ken-L Ration and attached articles about Davis. Lo and behold, Buster became one of ten dogs in the United States who's received a hero award: "Ken-L Ration was owned by Quaker Oats, but the brand was sold to H.J. Heinz Co. in 1995. Like several other dog food brands, Ken-L Ration issued a yearly award to brave or heroic dogs, titled the 'Ken-L Ration Dog Hero of the Year Award.' The last known year this was issued was 1996."[41]

John Beham

The funnel effect of floodwaters entering Lower Brady's Bend started at the Palmers' and then continued 150 yards to sixty-six-year-old John Beham's home and carpet shop. John was well known in the community, having installed new carpeting or flooring for many households. He was alone that evening and, like the Hendersons, was on his second floor during the highest water. He clung to his dog, utterly convinced that his end was near.

John's home rested amid the winding creek and in the narrowest part of the valley, between where Davis Palmer rescued Myrtle and Evelyn Ritchey, and the Custer house was lifted from its foundation.

Later, Beham reflected on his readiness to die when his house was lifted by the water. He thought, "I'm going. So, this is it." The house moved a few feet, then sat back down. The next morning, John's wife returned home, but John was nowhere to be found. She thought he had been washed away. An hour later, he came walking up the road and said, "I thought I was gone."

John Beham's home (*left*) and the carpet shop (*right*), August 15, 1980. *Jeff Olszak.*

That same luck was not on the side of those that were at the Custers' house, another 150 yards beyond Beham's home.

The Custer Home

The Custer home became a shelter for six people on the night of August 14, 1980. Elrick and Bertha (Elick and Birch) Custer lived there and often babysat their grandson Jerry Potts Jr.

That night, Betty Kaufman stopped for shelter at the Custers' on her way home from bingo. Carol Lege and Calvin Deemer (girlfriend and boyfriend) stopped on their return trip from Rimersburg, where they had set up Carol, a teacher, and her friend Patty's apartment for the start of the school year.

Elrick and Bertha (Elick and Birch) Custer and Jerry Potts Jr.

Elick and Birch Custer had lived in their Brady's Bend home since the 1960s. Their cherished quiet setting had Sugar Creek flowing behind it, and it was sheltered from the sight of even their closest neighbors. Their grandniece Tina Custer said, "They loved their little home and were very proud of it."

She remembers visiting them as a child for family picnics and gatherings and playing and swimming in their backyard creek.

Myrtle, Elick and Birch's only child, lived about half an hour from her parents. Even so, they were the trusted and loving caretakers for their two-year-old grandchild, Jerry Jr., during Myrtle's work week. Jerry Jr. often spent weekdays with his grandparents, with Myrtle picking him up on Friday.

The night of the flood was Thursday. Myrtle was due to pick up Jerry Jr. the following day.

Betty Kaufman

Betty Kaufman loved Thursday night bingo at East Brady Firehall. According to her daughter-in-law Glenda, who sometimes joined Betty, "Betty always liked to go and was especially excited because the jackpot had been increasing." Glenda recalled the evening of the flood; it had rained all week, and that day, it had stormed. Betty came to their house around 4:30 or 5:00 p.m. They had already eaten supper, and Glenda was outside on the back porch. Her husband, Mike, was working on his motorcycle in the yard. Betty asked Glenda to go to bingo, which started at 6:00 p.m. Glenda didn't want to go that night. Betty tried to talk her into going, but she still said no. Glenda and her family went into the house. Betty left on her own. Then it started raining.

Due to the storm, bingo ended early. The Ritcheys left and were in trouble below Davis Palmer's house. Betty Kaufman stopped for shelter at the Custers' home. She didn't know them, but they welcomed her in and offered the use of their phone. Betty called her youngest son, Rick, who lived at home, to let him know she was at the Custers', that she was alright and was going to stay there. Betty said bingo ended early, and although the firefighters encouraged people to stay, she decided to start home.

Betty's daughter Debbie and her husband, Randy, were at home canning beets that evening. After Rick got the call from Betty, he called Debbie who tried to reach her mother at the Custers'. The phone rang and rang with no one answering. She said, "We just couldn't understand why nobody was there." Randy hoped Betty was safe and that a downed electric or phone line was the problem.

Carol Lege and Calvin Deemer

From Leechburg, Pennsylvania, Carol Lege had been teaching at Union High School as a business teacher since graduating from Indiana University of Pennsylvania (IUP) the year prior. She shared an apartment in Rimbersburg (Union School District's hometown) with her friend Patty. Best friends since the ninth grade, Carol and Patty roomed together for their four years at IUP. Both had their hearts set on becoming teachers. After graduating from IUP, fate kept them together as teachers at Union School District.

During the school year, Carol and Patty roomed together in an apartment near the school. After that first school year ended, they returned to their families' Leechburg homes for the summer. Patty was taking a summer course at IUP, and Carol was back with her family, living closer to her boyfriend, Calvin.

On August 14, 1980, Carol asked Patty if she wanted to drive to Rimersburg with her and Calvin to get the apartment ready for the school year. Patty said no. She had a final exam Friday morning and was attending a concert in Pittsburgh later that day.

According to Paulette Lege (Dan Lege's wife), "The night of the flood, Carol called her parents from the Custer house. Carol and Calvin had pulled over and knocked on Custer's door. Then they called home to see what they should do." Paulette said that the people in the home were very kind. They told Carol and Calvin that it was no problem for them to stay. Carol called home around 11:00 p.m. The Leges later discovered that Carol's watch stopped at 11:11 p.m.

Carol's brother Dan had a strange experience shortly after 11:00 p.m. He got the worst headache he'd ever had in his life. He suffered with migraines but had never experienced anything like that. Paulette described Dan's usual migraines as those that came on slowly and lingered. This one hit like a bomb. Dan went from eating a bowl of cereal to suffering an excruciating migraine within seconds.

Dan reflected, "It was right about the time Carol was lost. By 11:11 I was—" Paulette ends Dan's sentence, "Throwing up. He was sick. Later, we realized that it happened at the same time Carol passed."

Friday morning, Paulette received a call at their home that Carol was missing. The caller suggested that they call their priest; that's when Paulette knew it was serious. Paulette called Dan; she didn't want him to drive home from work upset. She told him that she needed his help taking one of their daughters, who had an ear infection, to the doctor's office. When they arrived at the office, she told him about Carol.

Based on the call Paulette received, they didn't know if Carol was gone or simply lost. Some of Dan's coworkers offered to go to Brady's Bend to help Dan look for Carol.

Those Lost at the Custer Home

The only account we have from the Custer house is an interview with the sole survivor, Calvin Deemer, published in the August 18, 1980 edition of the *Post Gazette.*

> *Struggling in the pitch-dark night against the fury of rampaging Sugar Creek, Calvin Deemer clutched a tree limb.*
>
> *But as Deemer wrapped an arm around the life-saving branch, his girlfriend slipped from his other arm and was swept away.*
>
> *The 22-year-old steelworker from Apollo who hugged the limb for more than four hours before being rescued yesterday told of his narrow escape from death and recalled how the five others, including his girlfriend, barely missed surviving.*
>
> *Had they successfully made a 30-yard trek through the rising floodwaters, all six would have reached higher, safer ground, Deemer said.*
>
> *"We could have made it," he lamented.*
>
> *But moments after the group had turned back, the creek was out of control sweeping cars, chunks of road and uprooted trees downstream, ripping houses from their foundations and carrying almost everything in its path.*
>
> *Deemer and Miss Lege, who was preparing for her second year as a business teacher at Union Area High School, were trapped in the storm as they drove Route 68 toward her parents' home in Leechburg, Armstrong County.*
>
> *As they crossed the Allegheny River into Brady's Bend Township, the heavy rain intensified. It was about 10:15 p.m. when they decided to stop and wait out the storm, Deemer said.*
>
> *They sloshed through shoe-deep water to a nearby house to phone Miss Lege's parents, he said. A few minutes later they emerged from the house to find his Plymouth floating toward them in rising water.*
>
> *With the water deepening, the six decided to wade across the road to an embankment about 30 yards away, Deemer said. Behind the embankment, a hill led up to a trailer perched above the creek valley.*

"We stepped out in the water and made a chain. But [Custer] *fell in the water and we all grabbed for him and pulled him out, back to the house," Deemer said.*

They decided to wait.

As the water grew stronger and higher, Deemer believed a dam had broken. When Custer told him there was no dam, he felt relieved. "I figured it had to stop. The rain was slowing down a bit," he said.

Just then, they felt a jolt. The surging water had torn the house from its foundation.

"I grabbed my girlfriend and we ran out on the porch and jumped," Deemer said. "I knew that house wouldn't last much longer. The water was so swift it just took us away."

"We hit one tree and bounced off. It pulled us down to another tree with a vine hanging down, and I got a hand on it," he recalled. It was then that he felt his girlfriend of four years slip away.

At 2:45 a.m., after more than four hours, Deemer was still hanging on. Because of the darkness, he didn't realize the water had subsided until, "I saw this guy running up the road, where the water had been."[42]

The former location of the Custer home, August 15, 1980. *Jeff Olszak.*

At 2:45 a.m., Alfred McCanna found Calvin Deemer hanging from the tree. Alfred was out with his chainsaw. Once he was assured that his two daughters were safe, he was determined to help others. He and a friend began walking from their Seybertown homes through Brady's Bend. That's when they discovered Calvin.

Alfred helped Calvin down and took him to a nearby home. Calvin's entire body was covered in abrasions, and although he was still in shock, he recounted what happened.

Hester Lenora "Toni" Crissman

Not much is known about what Toni Crissman was doing the night she drowned in her home. She was sixty-seven and had just been released from the hospital using a walker. Her husband, Pete, was at St. Margaret's Hospital, admitted due to his own health concerns. The Crissman home sat within Sugar Creek's horseshoe, that last short stretch before it enters the Allegheny River.

Toni's brother lived along the Allegheny River, a few miles east of Toni's home, on Seybertown Road. During an interview with his son Bill, he admitted that his family didn't know anything had happened. They knew it had rained hard, but they had been watching the river to gauge the storm's impact. "It hadn't risen that much."

The next morning, Bill and a friend rode their bicycles down Seybertown Road to Brady's Bend. It was then that they finally realized how bad it was. By then, his dad was checking on Toni.

Campbell's Camp

Within the upper part of the same horseshoe but not visible from the Crissman house was Campbell's camp, which had been purchased by the family in 1955. The Campbells were known for their family-owned hardware store in East Brady. Established in the 1890s, the store transitioned to new ownership ninety years later and still exists today. The essential nature of this long-standing business has been its connection to the people in its rural community, allowing it to consistently outcompete big-box retailers.

The location of Arnie Frazier's cottage on the Campbell property. *David Cassesse.*

Brother and sister Bill and Terry Campbell were born and raised in East Brady and used the family camp as a getaway. During the summer as children, they admitted to spending more time at the camp than in their own home. On the camp property sat a second structure, a cottage rented by Arnie Frazier. Arnie was a well-known local leader who was famous for his photo as a World War II marine on the August 18, 1941 cover of *LIFE* magazine.

On August 14, Arnie was returning home during the hardest part of the rainstorm. He later told Terry that it was "a horrible drive." No sooner had Arnie pulled into the lane where his cottage stood than he heard the rushing water approaching from behind. According to Bill, Arnie was a smart guy. He immediately backed as far up the hillside as he could and then watched his cottage home be torn away.

Bill, who lived in Pittsburgh, heard about the flood and called Terry. She remembers him saying, "There's a flood." She said that she had heard about it. He responded, "No, you don't understand. There was a flood. People are dead. The cottage is gone. Arnie's place is gone. And our place was badly damaged."

Emergency Services' Response

East Brady Fireman Cliff Sigworth was working bingo on August 14 when the siren went off. Cliff recalled it first going off around 9:45 p.m. Responding to the siren, he crossed the parking lot from the firehall to the station. It was the Butler Control Center requesting the East Brady Fire Department's assistance with flooding in the nearby town of Petrolia.

As Cliff walked to the station, the rain was so intense that water surged over his shoes. He didn't know it yet, but in addition to Petrolia, Brady's Bend was also flooding.

He learned soon enough. While preparing to leave for Petrolia, the firemen received a call requiring a change in destination: Brady's Bend.

As Cliff and the fire crew prepared to respond, Fire Chief Corky Robinson and his wife were returning home to East Brady. Corky was determined to get to the firehall. He wanted to stop the bingo crowd from leaving. East Brady Fire Department bingo was popular for the small town. As many as seventy-five people attended. Many of them drove home directly through Brady's Bend.

As Corky left Butch Robinson's, water surged over his truck. He kept moving. Beyond Custer's house, he met his cousin Paul coming toward him. He hadn't stayed in East Brady as Corky had pleaded. As their vehicles met, they stopped. With the windows down, they began talking. At that same moment, a mound of earth nearly as high as their vehicles plummeted off the hillside. That's when Paul turned around.

When they arrived in East Brady, Corky asked a local cop to prevent people from crossing the river's bridge. It didn't close immediately, and the bingo crowd was let out.

Former East Brady Fireman Jim Curran went to the firehall that night to help get generators running and to keep the bingo players at the firehall. Jim said, "Some stayed. Some didn't."

By the time the firefighters had crossed the river bridge, they looked toward Sugar Creek. Cliff could see a chunk of pavement that had been washed from the roadway and was now lying on top of another. The first highway bridge was entirely flooded. The approach was washed out. Only the tops of each side barrier were visible. They couldn't cross. They didn't try. They were cut off. That's when they closed the Allegheny River bridge and prevented traffic from crossing into Brady's Bend.

Shortly before that closing, Evelyn and Myrtle Ritchey, Betty Kaufman, Carol Lege and Calvin Deemer crossed and drove on.

Typical destruction to the highway, August 15, 1980. *John Slick.*

When the water began receding, Cliff and another fireman began scanning the area with their flashlights. They saw a man hanging onto a tree not far away. With ropes in hand, they reached him and successfully lowered him to the ground. The man quickly left. To this day, Cliff does not know who the man was or where he had come from.

The firefighters summoned assistance from a local coal company, requesting its front loader. They needed it to move obstacles so they could enter Brady's Bend; chunks of pavement, trees, cars, parts of houses and garages were blocking their entry.

Help came quickly. The first equipment operator to arrive was familiar with the area. He knew detours, many of them dirt roads that skirted the main highway. Firefighters who knew the hillsides began hiking to access the community.

By daylight, the water had receded enough that more emergency response teams were able to begin hiking through in earnest. Climbing over and through obstructions, they slowly made their way deeper into the community.

At the upper end of Brady's Bend, Sugar Creek Fire Department was also encountering barriers to enter Brady's Bend. Three of that department's firefighters shared their experiences: Ernie Earley, Denny Cogley and Jimmy Hillwig Jr.

Ernie was co–fire chief in 1980, sharing the responsibility with Jimmy's father, Jim, who passed away in 2010 and had been a lifetime fireman. Jim Sr.'s obituary notes, "During the flood of 1980, Jim went nine days without rest trying to help those in need." Jimmy, following in his father's footsteps, was seventeen in 1980, a junior fireman. Denny was both a fireman and an ambulance driver.

Coincidentally, on the evening of August 14, the Sugar Creek firefighters were participating in a disaster training program at a local church when they received the call to help. They took their truck toward Kaylor (their quickest route to Brady's Bend). The final downhill stretch had water running across the roadway faster than their truck was able to move. Once in Kaylor, they stopped to rescue two people and their dogs from a flooded home. Ernie noted, "It was there that I lost my helmet. Three days later, it was found in the Allegheny River, over four miles away."

In Upper Brady's Bend, a truck was overturned on SR 68 with a wheelbarrow on top. *Tim Patsy.*

Leaving Kaylor, they soon discovered the roads were impassable. By now, surrounding fire departments were reaching out to each other, asking for or offering help. Sugar Creek firefighters realized that they needed to focus on Brady's Bend. Unable to enter with their vehicles, like the East Brady fireman, Sugar Creek's crew agreed that some firefighters would start walking the hillsides while others sought alternate routes.

While Ernie walked the hillside, Denny remained in Kaylor to provide a radio link. Denny admitted that the rushing water was so loud that he couldn't hear the radio and lost contact.

By then, other colleagues had driven their personal trucks to look for detour routes into Brady's Bend. The walking crews were the first to arrive in Upper Brady's Bend. There, they found two trucks upside down in the middle of SR 68, a foreshadowing of the devastation ahead.

As the floodwater began to recede, Jimmy Hillwig Jr. and his crew made their way down Poncic Hollow, adjacent to Holder Run. It was near daylight. They sat at the intersection of SR 68 and Poncic Hollow, facing the hillside. A huge portion of that hillside let loose. Its soil and trees nearly slid over their truck.

3

WHEN DAYLIGHT CAME

Before sunrise, Brady's Bend's residents were all in some degree of shock, still shrouded in fear and anxiety from the previous night. Rising from a few hours or no sleep, many wondered—or perhaps hoped—that the night had been nothing but a bad dream. Glancing out any window, the full disarray was still shadowed in partial darkness.

When daylight came, the reality was impossible to deny and nearly as impossible to take in. Most homes had basements full of water and mud. Some homes no longer existed. Yards were stripped clean and repainted with layers and layers of mud. The only exception was if something from upstream had landed there. The scale of damage to the area's trees, bushes, bridges and roads defied belief. Numb with shock, people started walking beyond their homes.

Joe Curran said that the sights made him feel like he was in a fog. Never in his life had he seen anything like it. Sugar Creek, normally six inches in depth, had transformed into a monster, causing unbelievable devastation. Family, friends and neighbors walked along what was left of SR 68, disoriented. There was no making sense of what they were seeing.

During Joseph Seybert's walk, he was awestruck by the power of the water. As a young civil engineering student, he was riveted by the impact on the small concrete bridges. When Joseph looked over what was left of the bridges, he noticed that the metal rebar reinforcement of the bridges' under-deck was exposed and had been forced downstream, extending eight to twelve feet in the air. Rushing water with abrasive gravel and debris had

Stunned residents walk along SR 68, surveying the damage and looking for victims. *James King Sr.*

scoured the concrete off and bent the rebar like it was nothing more than pipe cleaners.

In Lower Brady's Bend, where the valley narrows and the hillsides become steeper, the bridges were even worse. The undersides were scoured off completely. Even in places where the pavement above was intact, everything, including the rebar on each of the bridges' undersides, was gone.

Shoeless, Kelly McNaughton walked the two-and-a-half-mile trek to her East Brady home. She noticed the bridges, too, but for her, it wasn't the undersides that struck her, it was all the debris piled on top. They looked like mass-destruction war zones. Everything, from porches, piles of yard junk, chairs and swings, was stuck on the bridges. Cars that had made their way under the bridges came out the other side flattened, as if they had been through a crusher.

When Kelly stopped to talk to Joe Stimac, his face had a look of incomprehension. Kelly asked, "How's Carl?" Joe told her that he was fine, that they had gotten him upstairs with his oxygen. "By my God, look at this!"

As Kelly approached the elementary school, the playground still had its big swing set, but the schoolyard was covered with dogs, drowned dogs chained to their boxes. As residents struggled for their own survival, many didn't have

This car looks as if it has gone through a crusher, August 15, 1980. *Jeff Olszak.*

time to unchain their dogs. It was a bizarre scene. Ten or fifteen dogs' bodies were scattered throughout the schoolyard, some with their boxes nearby.

Across from the school, Kelly learned that one dog was saved that night. A couple who lived across the road told her that during the night, they were standing at the high point, alongside the bridge, when they heard a noise. Overcoming their own fear, they looked down and saw a crying dog. They grabbed its collar and pulled it up. At least one beagle lived that day, perhaps one let loose by Butch Robinson.

Many of those who walked around saw that the Custer house was gone, stripped away entirely. Jim Martin observed that the only remaining sign of the home was a foundation full of mud, like the remains of a historic ruin or an ancient civilization that he had seen at national parks. Matt Switzer said that although he moved away shortly after the flood, when he returns to Brady's Bend and drives past where the Custer house was, he is reawakened to everything that happened that night.

Surveying the damage, a common thought was, "Oh my God, how did anyone survive?" Some hadn't, and at that time, no one was exactly sure who and how many had perished. Many survivors also questioned whether they should have reacted differently, sought higher ground or stayed put rather than trying to drive.

The site where Sugar Creek entered the Allegheny River had become a huge sediment flat filled with cars, as if they had reached a finish line. No one knew how many or if any contained people.

Even more overwhelming than the damage was the smell. Nearly everyone described an overpowering revolting smell of mud and muck mixed with sewage. It was everywhere. Inescapable.

It was all so much worse than anyone could have imagined.

Searching for the Lost

After a night of the East Brady and Sugar Creek firefighters struggling to find ways to enter Brady's Bend, the morning presented new challenges. Crews started going door to door, from brush pile to brush pile. They investigated basements, many with their lights on and full of water. They were looking for survivors and victims alike.

Fireman Corky Robinson said that "locating people was our biggest issue." They didn't know who was missing, who might have climbed a hillside or gotten picked up by a friend or family. Gradually, people started talking as word came in that this person or that person was missing.

The search extended through Brady's Bend to the Allegheny River, with boaters searching the river and its banks. Soon, dozens of fire crews from surrounding communities arrived to help. Because of the amount of debris, the going was slow, covering and clearing as little as a quarter of a mile each day. Many firefighters worked nonstop for the first forty-eight hours, taking catnaps before resuming their efforts.

For local emergency personnel, knowing the community and its members was a blessing and curse. In a place where everybody knew everybody and were often related to each other, concerns about who and what they would discover were haunting. Would it be a relative or neighbor?

Even more troubling was when the volunteers learned that they were looking for at least two children. Sugar Creek Co–Fire Chief Ernie Early acknowledged that during his search, he found several baby dolls among the wreckage. His heart skipped a beat each time.

East Brady Fire Chief Corky Robinson said that searching for people during those first couple of days was terrible. Although they were numb, they kept going. When they could go on no more, they rested in a corner, their minds never stopping. When they went home to sleep, some dreamed of the flood. After a few hours of sleep, most awoke with their minds racing.

On Friday, a command and relief center was established at St. Patrick's Church's social hall.[43] The church itself took the brunt of the flood, with three stained-glass windows destroyed. Water and mud had reached the altar. The social hall, protected by the church, was quickly converted into a command center for help, information and coordination. Each day, emergency personnel met there and organized efforts. Assignments were divided by area. The community placed a large banner of support over the social hall's doors: "We Bend But We Don't Break." Governor Dick Thornburg visited the site in the first few days, pledging to help in the cleanup.[44]

Volunteers search from brush pile to brush pile for the lost. *Tim Boltz.*

St. Patrick's Church, with its social hall's command center, was protected from major damage. *David Cassesse.*

With chainsaws to clear brush, the crews spent hours cutting, digging and removing trees and rubbish. Residents with special equipment were enlisted. After towing several cars to a central location, Andy Seybert remembers the state police arriving on Friday. One officer summoned Andy to bring his tow truck to search for bodies in cars. They moved along Sugar Creek to the river. While most cars were pulled free, an unreachable car in the middle of the creek was left for heavy equipment extraction. Whether someone was in the car had to be left for later.

Next to where the Custer home had been, there were two cars stuck in a ravine. While there, Andy couldn't help but wonder what had caused the house to become dislodged from its foundation and wash away. Puzzled, he looked at the steep hillside across the creek, behind where the house had been. What he saw put the home's fate into perspective. A large avalanche had fallen off the hillside into the creek. Although he didn't know the landslide's timing, it was easy to imagine that it could have compounded the devasting force of the floodwater and debris, further condemning the house and its refugees.

As hard as search teams worked, it took five days before all nine of those who perished were found. The last was found on Tuesday, August 19. Two-year-old Jerry Potts Jr. was found fifteen miles to the south in the Allegheny River near the town of Templeton.

Four other victims were found in the river. On Friday, Birch Custer was found at the coal tipple across from the town of East Brady. Betty Ellen Robinson was found five miles south of East Brady, near the community of Wattersonville. Later that day, Betty Kaufman was found an unbelievable twenty-eight miles south of East Brady, near the town of Manorville. On Monday, August 18, twenty-two-year-old Carol Lege was found at the lower end of East Brady, about a mile from where Sugar Creek enters the Allegheny River.

During the first day of searching, Friday, August 15, Butch Robinson was found caught in a tree below Queenstown Road. Elick Custer was found near the mouth of Sugar Creek. And four-year-old Amy Robinson was found in Wilson and Catherine Downing's garage, a little over half a mile from where the Robinson truck had fallen into Sugar Creek.

As the Downing family surveyed damage, their two sons saw their father's new, now-beat-to-a-pulp wheelbarrow near the elementary school. They walked down as a family to retrieve it. Their fourteen-year-old son, John, offered to wheel it home. When he arrived, he took the wheelbarrow to their garage behind the home. There, he found Amy Robinson lying over their lawnmower in the corner of the garage. Ambulance driver Denny Cogley said the memory of removing Amy from the garage and transporting her to the morgue was heartbreaking. It's something he will never forget.

While surveying the damage caused suffering, the anguish was cruelest for the family members who knew their loved ones were lost but didn't yet know their fate. Five of the nine who were lost were from the Custer home.

Elick and Birch Custer and Jerry Potts Jr.

Like many others stranded in Brady's Bend that Thursday night, Tina (Custer) Sullivan returned to her East Brady home the next morning. She knew her great-uncle and -aunt and their grandson, Jerry, were missing and that their house was gone. None had yet been found. Although she felt unsettled and afraid of the prospect of finding a body, she put on her grandfather's wading boots and joined her cousins as they walked to Brady's Bend.

It was an eerie feeling, wondering if she was strong enough for what she might see. Her ordeal at the Brady's Bend Hotel and not knowing the fate of her relatives produced a complex mix of emotions.

She recalled seeing a community of people park their cars at the East Brady end of the river bridge. On foot, they crossed the bridge, most of them with the intention of helping in whatever way possible.

Tina couldn't shake her unease. A quarter of a mile before the Custer property, she noticed a lone dishwasher. The incongruity of seeing a dishwasher outside was like most everything she saw that day: bizarre. Prepared to investigate, she put her gloves on and opened the dishwasher. Inside were her aunt's jewel-tone aluminum cups. She remembered those same cool-to-the-touch cups hurting her teeth during dinners at her great-uncle and great-aunt's house.

Tina had had enough. She turned back and went home.

Terry Campbell, another East Brady resident, walked toward her family's camp. It was down the road from where the Custers' home had been. Although she hadn't yet heard who was missing, she began her walk with an unnerving feeling. She met friends who were coming the other direction, and they were all wondering the same: "What happened here?!"

When Terry arrived at the Campbell camp's lane, she saw what appeared to be a random car. On top of its hood was a photo album with loose pictures.

She glanced at them. It was the Custers'. It wasn't until later that she learned they were missing and presumed drowned.

Myrtle Custer (Jerry's mother and Elick and Birch's daughter) made it to Brady's Bend on Friday. Both of her parents were found that day. As she waited for news about her son, she planned and held the funeral for her parents that following Monday. On Tuesday, Jerry Jr. was found.

Betty Kaufman

While Betty was sheltering with the Custers, she called her son Rick, who soon spread the word of her plight to family members. They were experiencing intense anxiety because of their inability to reach the Custer house by phone. Some of the family waited overnight in Upper Brady's Bend. By daybreak, Betty's husband, Walt, son Mike and son-in-law Randy were walking through Brady's Bend, searching for Betty. As they surveyed the damage, they realized that the Custer home must have been the farthest Betty could have gone before stopping.

With an incredulity at what they were seeing and smelling, they kept moving. They saw a heavy-set, black-haired woman from the back and thought it was Betty. They had found her! Mike called, "Mom!" The woman turned around. It wasn't Betty.

When they arrived at the place where the Custer house had been, they saw Betty's car against a tree. Their lives had become a nightmare.

Eventually, they went to Betty and Walt's home. Later that evening, they received a call from the coroner letting the family know that they believed they had found Betty—in the river, twenty-eight miles south of East Brady. They needed a family member to identify the body at the hospital morgue. Walt and their uncle went inside the hospital, while Debbie and Randy waited in the car. It was Betty.

Contributing to their nightmare was their search for a funeral home. Local funeral homes weren't accustomed to serving so many at one time, yet the Kaufmans found one. Betty's funeral was scheduled for the following Monday.

Carol Lege

Carol had called her parents the evening prior to let them know she and Calvin were safe at the Custers' home. The family didn't hear anything more until the next morning, when Paulette Lege received the call that let them know Carol was missing—and that suggested they call their priest.

Carol's roommate and fellow teacher, Patty (McConville) DeBiasio, received a call from Dan Lege on Friday morning. He asked if she had heard from Carol. She had not. That's when he told her about the flood. Feeling she needed to do something, she and a friend went to Carol's parents' home. After receiving no news for some time, Patty and her friend drove to East Brady. They made it as far as the East Brady Firehall before they were told that they could not enter Brady's Bend.

Friday morning, Dan, Paulette and Dan's uncle drove from Leechburg to Brady's Bend to seek news and look for Carol. Awestruck by the destruction, Dan noticed insects crawling on the ground; he wondered how something so small could survive the disaster while people had not. During Dan and Paulette's search, Paulette found Carol's purse, and Dan found her car—now unrecognizable to Paulette.

Like Myrtle Custer, who was waiting for news about her son, Jerry, the Leges returned home, wondering if there was reason to have faith that Carol might still be found safe.

When Carol was found on Monday, the Leechburg undertaker advised Dan to let him identify her, since he knew her and the family well. That same undertaker gave them Carol's watch, which had stopped at 11:11 p.m.

The Robinsons

Butch, Betty Ellen and Amy Robinson were all discovered on Friday. East Brady firefighters found Butch tangled in a tree. Amy was found by John Downing in his family's garage. It is unknown who discovered Betty Ellen in the river. What we do know is that boaters were looking for victims, and many others were walking the riverbanks.

Betty Ellen's parents, the Liases, had sheltered Tom "T-Turtle" in their truck that night. Like others whose homes had been severely damaged or washed away, the Liases were provided temporary housing by family and friends until the federal government could provide them a home in a temporary trailer. Sixteen-year-old T-Turtle lost his father, mother and sister. His entire family. His family's home had been washed away. His grandparents' home was so badly damaged, it was unlivable. T-Turtle shifted from house to house until the Downings stepped in. T-Turtle was a day older than the Downings' oldest son. They were friends. Catherine Downing contacted T-Turtle's grandmother and offered to keep him until the Liases were settled. T-Turtle lived with them for the next month.

During that time, T-Turtle told the Downings that he had looked for signs of his family in the flood debris. All he found was a sheet and one of his sister's toys.

Toni Crissman

On Friday, as the East Brady firefighters began their search for victims and survivors, twenty-three-year-old Firefighter Jim Curran arrived at Toni Crissman's house. He knew that Toni's husband, Pete, was in St. Margaret's Hospital in Pittsburgh, because Pete was roommates with Jim's brother. Toni had been home alone.

Toni's nephew said that Toni had been recently released from the hospital and was using a walker.

Searching with a local EMT volunteer, Jim broke through the living room window to enter the home. Looking at the walls, he noticed a water mark that was nearly as high as his head. The room was full of mud and muck. Unbelievably, a box fan was still running and caused Jim an electric shock. The couch was turned upside down, and when he looked behind it, he saw Toni lying on the floor beside her overturned walker.

4

CLEANUP AND RECOVERY

It's not often that a community of just over one thousand makes national news. Yet coverage of the Brady's Bend flood reached far and wide. With friends across the United States because of her military career, retired Lieutenant Colonel Betty Cassesse had scrapbooks that contained articles that were sent to her from across the United States, including Topeka, Kansas; Mentor and Youngstown, Ohio; and San Diego, California. The same Associated Press article that was picked up in Betty's friends' towns was also run in the *Washington Post*, *New York Times*, *Philadelphia Inquirer* and *Los Angeles Times*.

Friday morning, the Sugar Creek and East Brady Fire Departments continued their painstaking search and cleanup. As the word spread, they were joined by a cadre of local fire companies.

Beyond discovering damage, people were propelled outside by their worry over the fate of their family and friends. Even those who had experienced the worst of the destruction didn't take long to galvanize. After assessing the damage to their own homes, many yearned to know about others. The not-knowing caused feelings ranging from worry to terror. Because most phones weren't working, the only way to find information was to walk. Amid the shock of what they were seeing and an increasing anxiety about what might be ahead, people had the compulsion to move forward.

The destruction of roads and bridges and the sights of homes moved from their foundations and cars in piles of other debris caused many to ask, "How did anyone survive?" Some, like Amy Miller, started out early

Typical roadway and bridge damage. *James King, Sr.*

in the morning. Anxious to get to her five-month-old son at her parents' home, her uncle and cousin's husband guided her through water that was still running swiftly enough to lift her off her feet. In another instance, when Helen Bartoe saw the condition of her brother Scabby's house. She couldn't believe anyone had survived.

Ann Bratkovich (now Stanley) was scheduled to be married at St. Patrick's Church the following Saturday, August 23. On Friday, she joined others in walking the distance of Brady's Bend with a special interest in St. Patrick's Church. She soon became a bride who had to adjust every plan she'd made for her wedding just eight days away.

She was speechless at what she saw when she opened the church's doors, and she realized immediately that there was no way it would be ready for her wedding the following Saturday. As soon as she returned home, she began the arduous process of finding a new church and reception hall. The neighboring Catholic church was available, but finding a reception hall took many more calls. Once she confirmed a new hall, she began calling her caterer, DJ and organist/soloist to note the venue changes. Then came the mammoth task of informing her invitees, some of whom were not able make it, as they were recovering from the flood themselves.

Ann E. Bratkovich
and
Howard P. Stanley
invite you to share in the joy
when they exchange marriage vows
and begin their new life together
on Saturday, the twenty-third of August
Nineteen hundred and eighty
at twelve noon
St. Patrick's Roman Catholic Church
Brady's Bend, Pennsylvania

Reception following ceremony
until 6 p.m.
St. Patrick's Hall

Ann Stanley with her husband, Howard "Bud" Stanley, August 23, 1980. *Ann Stanley*.

Betty Custer's car several yards below Brady's Bend Hotel. *Tim Patsy*.

Upturned railroad tracks at Blue Row Coal Tipple, August 15, 1980. *Florence DeBacco.*

As people walked through Brady's Bend, they shared the location of each other's cars: "It's in a pile of debris at St. Patrick's Church. It's in Andreassi's backyard. It's behind Seybert's. It's sitting against so and so's house."

More than one refrigerator was found. One was resting high against downed trees at the Campbells' camp. The Andreassis' was found several hundred yards from their home, identified by the family's pictures of their children still sticking to its door. Residents found their freezers, washers and dryers bobbing in their basements. Some were salvageable, but most were not. During their walks, people retrieved possessions that had been washed from their homes—riding mowers, go-carts, fishing boats, wheelbarrows, tools, toys, bicycles and porch chairs.

The railroad encountered major destruction. Bessemer & Lake Erie Railroad's track stopped in Upper Brady's Bend at Blue Row Tipple. Incredibly, the last two miles of its track had been twisted from its bed. The fallen railroad trestle that had taken out Millionaire Row's garages was now a stack of ties protecting Pezzuti's store.

U.S. Army Corps of Engineers

The day after the flood, technicians from the U.S. Army Corps of Engineers arrived from Pittsburgh's district office. Werner C. Loehlein, PE, PLS, DWRE, a retired chief of water management for the Pittsburgh district office of the U.S. Army Corps of Engineers (the Corps) remembers the Brady's Bend flood. In 2016, he retired after forty-four years of participating in flood investigations, supervising the release of water from federal reservoirs and completing hydrometeorological and water quality data collection and modeling. He currently lectures and designs curriculum in water resources engineering at the University of Pittsburgh's Swanson School of Engineering.

Loehlein, who completed several flood investigations, recalled "an avalanche of floods that occurred between 1972 and 1990, including 1972 Hurricane Agness and 1977 Johnstown Flood."

In 2024, Loehlein described the role of the Corps when a flood or highwater event like the one in Brady's Bend occurred. Typically, a team of field technicians were sent to the site to (1) define the extent of flooding due to overbank (out of stream) flooding by identifying highwater marks and (2) assess the damage to public facilities such as roads, bridges, highways and water and sewage systems.

This data is needed to support a governor's application for a federal disaster declaration. The disaster declaration provides a wide range of federal assistance programs for individuals and public infrastructure (such as roadways and bridges), including funds for both emergency and permanent work. Beyond this, individuals may be eligible for low-interest loans and temporary housing. Since most counties and states have limited resources, a federal disaster declaration is a critical step in supplementing the local and state responses. The goal of any disaster response is to restore things back to normal by doing things like dredging a channel to its original capacity.

Beyond helping local communities validate a flood's impact, the Corps' data gathering helps evaluate the effectiveness of its own flood control projects like the construction of reservoirs, bridges, highways and water and sewage systems.

Loehline remembered the reaction of the technician who was sent to survey the damage in Brady's Bend. At no time during the technician's drive did he see anything that prepared him for what he would see when he entered Brady's Bend. He told Loehline, "It was crazy! Devastating!"

HELP ARRIVES

The number of individuals and agencies who arrived to help is something that all the residents remember. Not everyone knew who was helping, only that there were a lot of people, agencies, volunteers, groups and businesses who came.

Backhoes, skid loaders, dump trucks, bulldozers and water trucks arrived. Neighbors were helping neighbors; families were helping families. It was a time when the slights of the past were put aside, replaced by a spirit of generosity.

An immediate need was cleanup. A dump location was identified, expanding an already existing dump on Schultz's Kittanning Hollow property. As basements were emptied, debris was removed from bridges and creek banks, loose pavement and concrete was taken from the roadways and railroad ties were hauled from upturned tracks and destroyed trestles, the mountains of trash needed to go somewhere. Schultz's pit became a bustling place.

Every home benefitted from the help of the fire companies and the U.S. Army Reserves 319th Engineer Company, part of the 99th ARCOM (Army

One home's basement trash ready for pickup. *Joni (King) Steiner.*

U.S. Army Reserves 319th Engineering Company support clean-up. *Sugar Creek Fire Department.*

Command). Brady's Bend resident Bruce Bly was a reservist in the 319th Company, and the weekend following the flood, he was due to participate in his monthly drill schedule. A decision to have his unit assist with flood recovery was made by the local command. Fortunately, the 319th Company was one that trained with heavy equipment (bulldozers, front-end loaders, dump trucks and a high-pressure water truck).

That first weekend, the reservists, with their heavy equipment, were in Brady's Bend assisting with all aspects of the cleanup. For another few weeks, reservists who were eligible for additional training hours continued to help. The water truck, dump truck and loader remained in Brady's Bend until September's monthly drill. Until then, Bruce, as a volunteer driver with a group of local volunteers, continued the grueling cleanup.

The generosity of 319th Company mimicked that of so many others, especially that of the volunteer firefighters. A resounding sentiment was that the local fire departments were incredible. With Sugar Creek and East Brady firefighters in the forefront, they tag-teamed with their high-pressure water trucks and Bruce's volunteers as they worked their way through the entirety of Brady's Bend. For ten days, they sprayed over eighty-nine basements and drains. At that point, many volunteers were required to return to work.

Above: Local fire companies assisted wherever needed. *David Cassesse.*

Left: Vincent Bartoe's volunteer pin and badge. *Vincent L. Bartoe.*

More than one resident commented on the tireless commitment of these volunteers. When another hard rain hit a week after the flood, at least a few basements needed cleaning again.

Local youth, too, became volunteers. Vince Bartoe, the son of Helen Bartoe, was fourteen years old and at home with his mother during the flood. After a visit from Governor Thornburg, who was seeking volunteers in the cleanup effort, Vince and other youth stepped up and were given official volunteer badges. They helped until they had to return to school two weeks later.

When the sun came out, the mud dried and turned into interminable clouds of dust that penetrated everything. In an endless battle, firefighters' water trucks often moved up and down roadways, spraying them to keep them wet. One fireman described the feeling of futility in addressing the dust. No matter how often they wet the ground's surface, the dust soon returned, trying everyone's patience. Eventually, the state brought in industrial-size street sweepers for a more permanent solution.

Johnstown volunteers, who had experienced the 1977 flood just three years earlier, touched the hearts of residents and firefighters alike. While talking with the Johnstown group, Firefighter Cliff Sigworth explained to them that they had found the bodies and no longer needed help with search and rescue. The Johnstown group told him that they hadn't come for that. They came to help with the cleanup, bringing their own tools and supplies for a back-breaking job. These selfless individuals wanted only to relieve the misery that they themselves knew.

Florence DeBacco said the first people at her door were people from Johnstown with buckets, mops, brushes and shovels. They understood what residents were going through and what they needed most.

Dave Cassesse remembers the deep emotion of saying goodbye when the Johnstown crews finally returned home. Grown men stood in his family's driveway crying. Twenty-four years old at the time, as he reflected on that moment, he was still moved by the impact of those generous helpers. Lifelong friendships developed between the Brady's Bend families and those from Johnstown. Christmas cards were exchanged for years. The simple but exhausting act of cleaning basements and yards for strangers brought grown men to tears.

The Salvation Army and Red Cross set up at the St. Patrick's command center, where they helped provide food, cleaning supplies, lost eyewear and IDs, inoculations for emergency workers and funds for clothing and household items.

Many residents were disoriented from the overwhelming sights, smells and losses. Monica Andreassi who lost her purse and eyeglasses described the ordeal as being "a very odd time" as she was guided through the steps of replacing her lost ID and eyewear. She realized she would never be able replace the pictures of her father that had been tucked in her wallet.

Beyond these disaster support groups, food came from a bounty of sources—enough to provide three hot meals a day for two weeks for residents and workers. The Sugar Creek and East Brady Women's Auxiliaries and local church groups made and delivered dozens of meals. The Red Cross contracted with Shop 'n Save in East Brady to prepare and deliver meals.[45] Individuals sent canned goods and produce from their gardens. Eventually,

WATER

The water tankers will be distributing red flags to homeowners today. These flags will designate which homes need drinking water. You should display them in a prominent place like your front porch, if you need water, so that it can be easily seen from the road. Please leave your containers on the porch so that the men can easily fill them. If you are physically unable to move the container, the men will come to the door to fill it.

THE BRADY AREA MINISTERIUM
Box 487
East Brady
Pennsylvania 16028

DEAR FRIENDS,

YOUR NEIGHBORS HAVE GATHERED A LIMITED AMOUNT OF FINANCIAL ASSISTANCE TO AID VICTIMS OF THE RECENT FLOOD. SINCE YOU MAY HAVE EXPERIENCED DAMAGE, WE ARE ENCLOSING AN APPLICATION FORM FOR THIS AID. IF YOU REQUIRE ASSISTANCE, PLEASE FILL OUT THE FORM AND RETURN IT BY <u>SEPTEMBER 1, 1980</u> TO ANY LOCAL PASTOR, OR MAIL IT TO:

BRADY AREA MINISTERIUM
BOX 487
EAST BRADY, PA. 16028

PLEASE REMEMBER THAT FUNDS ARE LIMITED. ALL APPLICATIONS WILL BE PROCESSED ON OR AFTER SEPTEMBER 1, 1980.

OUR PRAYERS ARE WITH YOU, IN JESUS' NAME

THE BRADY AREA MINISTERIUM

Top: Fresh water announcement. *David Cassesse.*

Bottom: Aid from the Brady Area Ministerium announcement. *David Cassesse.*

the two weeks' worth of hot meals from various sources ended, and the Salvation Army set up a mobile canteen at St. Patrick's Church.[46]

Drinking water tankers provided residents with flags to display on their front porch to indicate they needed their sanitary water containers refilled.

Catholic Charities, the Brady Area Ministerium (leaders from all faiths) and local banks provided funds. A benefit dance with volunteer bands and other entertainment was sponsored by a nearby community Moose Lodge and area merchants.

Coordinated by the Pennsylvania Department of Community Affairs with federal funds, a thirty-pad mobile home park was built in Brady's Bend, providing temporary housing for residents whose homes were unlivable or had been destroyed. Businesses had as much or more to clean up. Yet even local businesses and manufacturers gave their employees time off to assist the communities with cleanup.

Rebuilding

By mid-September, the first Brady's Bend Township Water and Sewer Authority was established to usher in a new age with a township sewage treatment plant. Until this point, Brady's Bend had a series of sewage collection tanks at various locations. My family's yard served as the collection point for all the families in the upper end of Brady's Bend. Three tanks were buried beneath one of our play areas. The flood demonstrated the threat of such a design. The overtaxed tanks backed up into our already flooded basement.

It was a problem with some urgency, and my father and oldest brothers dug a twenty-foot-long trench from our basement to the creek bank and then knocked concrete blocks from the basement wall to drain it. When the tanks continued to back up into our home with the entirety of Upper Brady's Bend's raw sewage and toilet paper floating freely, another trench was dug from the tanks to the creek. Their sides were broken open to drain them, too. This was not a sanitary or environmentally friendly solution, particularly when viewed from the 2020s, but it was a survival solution at that time.

While most interactions between neighbors were exceedingly generous, the draining of the sewage tanks brought one neighbor to our home to complain about my father's efforts. My dad, who had earlier told one of his Olszak Garage customers to not worry about paying his bill given everyone's circumstances, said to the complaining neighbor, "You can stay here and talk about the Steelers or the Pirates, but if you're going to talk about this, get the hell out." The neighbor left.

Until the sewer system was in place, portable toilets were scattered throughout the community. Another stopgap effort was a lime distribution center that was set up at the command center. Here, residents obtained lime to "counteract the odor of malfunctioning septic tanks and prevent the spread of disease."[47]

One week after the flood, on August 21, 1980, President Carter declared parts of Armstrong County (including Brady's Bend), Butler and Clarion Counties a federal disaster area.[48] This made funds available through the Federal Emergency Management Agency (FEMA) and low-interest loans through the Small Business Administration (SBA). Many families took advantage of low-interest SBA loans to repair their homes, essentially taking on a second mortgage. Volunteer fire companies were also eligible to receive a reimbursement of $11.50/hour of labor for each piece of equipment used.[49]

These low-interest loans were desperately needed, because many Brady's Bend homeowners did not have flood insurance, even though the National Flood Insurance Program (NFIP) had been established in 1968. In 1979, the Carter administration strengthened NFIP with Executive Order 12127, which established the Federal Emergency Management Agency (FEMA). NFIP was placed under FEMA's jurisdiction. According to a Wikipedia article, NFIP has two purposes: "to share the risk of flood losses through flood insurance and to reduce flood damages by restricting floodplain development."[50]

It wasn't until 1986 that FEMA conducted a flood insurance study of Brady's Bend Township, identifying flood zones, thereby establishing properties prone to flooding.[51] Those anticipated to flood within a one-hundred-year timeframe, were required to carry flood insurance. Typically, when a property changed hands, the mortgage lender would require flood insurance to be purchased. Depending on the lender, flood insurance may also be required for areas with more moderate risk (floods that were anticipated to occur every one hundred to five hundred years).

Today, NFIP is considered "broke and beleaguered,"[52] with many homeowners discontinuing their coverage due to the rising rates.[53] Owing to the swelling costs of damages, particularly related to the increase in the annual number of coastal hurricanes, insurance providers are also discontinuing flood insurance for some of their customers.

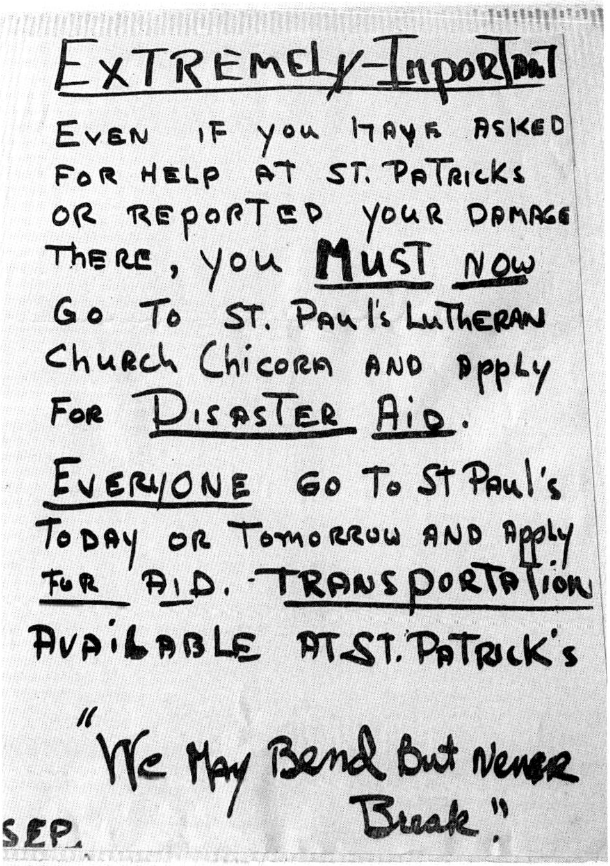

Flyer announcing federal aid. *David Cassesse.*

By the end of August 1980, contracts for debris removal had been awarded through the U.S. Department of Agriculture Soil Conservation Service. Contractors moved quickly. Debris removal was required within seven days. Major riprapping, the use of large loose stones to rebuild and protect the ground from erosion on creek banks and nearby bridges, was to be completed within thirty days.

Several residents noticed that the erosion exposed bedrock on the creek's bottom and had widened the creek in many places. Often, the change ate away at families' yards that were never returned to their former contour.

Another major task was the recovery and removal of residents' automobiles, most of which were declared totaled. Firefighter Ernie Early said that nearly twenty were pulled from the mouth of the river, with more gathered throughout Brady's Bend. As residents waited for insurance settlements, many cars were towed to local dealership properties or to the

Riprapping occurred at bridges and on eroded creek banks. *David Cassesse.*

Cars retrieved from the Allegheny River and Brady's Bend. They were towed to an East Brady dealership property and remained there until they could be assessed by insurance. *Marylin Kay Weibel.*

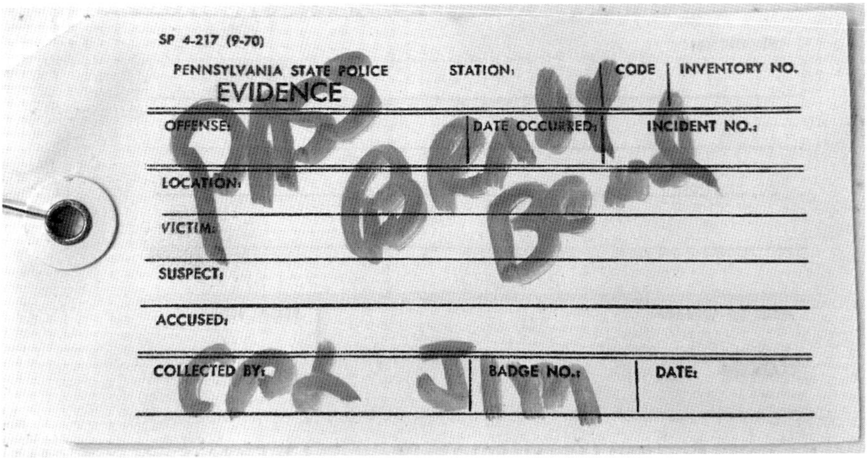

A permit allowing entrance into Brady's Bend. *David Cassesse.*

property of the original owner before they eventually made their way to the junkyard.

Opening the roadway was an urgent need. By August 29, at least one lane was open, but the entire road was closed from 8:00 a.m. to 5:00 p.m. for cleanup crews. The only exceptions to the closure were the school buses that returned between 2:30 p.m. and 3:15 p.m.[54] One-way traffic control for the construction site consisted of handing a flag to the last driver in the line of traffic. Only local traffic was allowed, and residents were required to hang a permit from their rearview mirror.

Five-year-old Harry Bortmes remembers how exciting it was to be the one who held the flag. Each flag holder was tasked with handing it back to the worker on the other side. Some drivers drove right on by, admitting that they forgot to return it.

The bridge and roadway repairs were completed within four months, and SR 68 was fully reopened.

Amazingly, school started on time, although Brady's Bend Elementary School never reopened. Instead, those elementary students were sent to neighboring Sugar Creek Elementary. With only a handful of central locations for bus stops, Brady's Bend youth walked some distance from their homes to catch the bus. Before the school year started, bus drivers practiced navigating through roadway construction.

Resident Betty Cassesse summed up the challenges and progress in her 1980 Christmas letter. She created three scrapbooks with the most complete and extensive collection of photos (with descriptions, dates, headings and, in some cases, time of day), local and national news articles (from friends across the nation), travel passes and announcements of all sorts. Her Christmas letter is one of the items within a scrapbook.

> *Betty Cassesse's Christmas Letter, December 1980*
>
> *It has been a most memorable year for us. One in which we have experienced joy, sorrow, fear and most of all—Thanksgiving that the Good Lord has seen fit to have us here at all. Our quiet, often dull days have become busy with efforts to restore order and some semblance of normality to our lives....*
>
> *On August 14, our world was turned topsy-turvy by a devastating flood. In less than one hour starting at 10 p.m.; 9 lives were lost, 12 homes were totally destroyed and the other 89 suffered varying degrees of damage. Great chunks of real estate were washed away taking with them the water and sewage systems in the village. Roads were impassable either due to mudslides, debris or destruction.*
>
> *Now 2½ months later we still have Porta-Potties dotting the landscape. Running water has been restored but is still not drinkable.*
>
> *Construction began October 30 on a new water treatment supply plant and a sewage treatment plant. These are due for completion within 90 days, more or less.*
>
> *We consider ourselves very lucky to be alive and we were able to stay in our home while damages were repaired.*
>
> *Sam* [Betty's husband] *has assumed a major burden as Treasurer of the newly formed Water and Sewer Authority. They had to start from scratch setting up books to accommodate all the red tape which comes with funding through State and Federal Agencies.*
>
> *Betty, with her big mouth, got involved with Community Action for the Villages; serves as secretary for Sam in his treasurer's job and is generally enjoying the activity. Just to get away she also helps with various Red Cross Bloodmobiles in the county once a month....*
>
> *To those who called or wrote after seeing Brady's Bend make the National News Releases, "Thanks for caring." The moral support was a big boost following the fear, depression and the Mud. Mud. Mud.*
>
> *We hope that you are all well and that the Good Lord will bless you with a Happy Holiday and bountiful New Year.*

Ninety days was an ambitious goal for completion of the water and sewage treatment plant. Instead, it was completed in August 1981.[55]

Forced to use a portable toilet, retired army Lieutenant Colonel Betty Cassesse maintains a sense of humor. *David Cassesse.*

Tragedy Brings a Community Together

Beyond agencies and volunteers, people noticed one another. Families helped families, and others helped in whatever way they could. A young mother at the time, Marilyn Magnani described, "Instead of individuals, everybody became one. It was neat. People that I only said hello to came to my house and said, 'What do you need done? What can I help you with?' It made me realize how times of stress and need make people closer and more willing to help."

Many others expressed similar sentiments of wonder at how well people banded together to help one another. Kelly McNaughton reflected, "It was amazing how much people contributed, especially food. A case of cabbage or bushel of tomatoes. The women at St. Patrick's cooked all day long, three meals a day." Neighbors who were struggling to clean their own homes made extra meals so they could share them with neighbors who were worse off. Families who received food donations from friends and family took some to St. Patrick's to share with others. Two survivors, Chris Henderson and

Barry Robinson, expressed nearly identical sentiments: "It's amazing how much human kindness emerged from that flood."

Teenager Matt Bartoe's friends from a neighboring town came to the Bartoe family's home to clean their basement. Joseph Seybert's out-of-town girlfriend's family brought meals to him and his family. Cousins chipped in to replace Tina Custer's dorm supplies and drop her off at college. Several volunteers and patrons helped Pezzuti's local store and Brady's Bend Hotel restore their businesses. Volunteers celebrated when they learned that Pezzuti's antique wine press was saved.

Businesses also helped. Tony Pezzuti from Brady's Bend Hotel offered workers sandwiches and sealed soda pop or beer. Firefighter Ernie Early said that the locals' independent streak demonstrated itself when someone from the state health department told Mr. Pezzuti that he wasn't permitted to hand out drinks that had been flooded, even if they had remained sealed. The health department worker was chased off. In another case, the firefighter auxiliary volunteers were told that they weren't permitted to used home-canned products in their meal preparation, so they hid them from authorities by taking them through the back door at St. Patrick's Social Hall and into the kitchen.

American Hardware, a dealer-owned wholesale hardware company in nearby Butler, donated a variety of supplies. Many of the company's employees lived in the Brady's Bend and Chicora areas.

Mary Ronge, whose home sat high enough that it wasn't flooded, took her dehumidifier to the Mellish home. Unfortunately, that same dehumidifier demonstrated one of a small number of incidents where someone tried to take advantage of the catastrophe. In this instance, a man entered the Mellish home and began to walk away with the dehumidifier. On his way out, he was seen and stopped by Mrs. Mellish. Residents were also warned to be careful of out-of-towners who were trying to establish repair contracts that required downpayments and then disappearing.

EPILOGUE

When I started this project, I was curious about the consequences of such a traumatic event on people's lives, particularly after forty-four years. I asked my interviewees, "Do you think your experience of the flood changed the way you think about or approach life?"

One thing was clear, talking about their experiences resurfaced strong emotions. At times, I wondered if revisiting such a deeply emotional experience was asking too much. Two interviewees said that it was healing for them. In 2024, they revisited a time in their life (1980) from a different perspective, feeling enough distance from the event to look at pictures, yearbooks or notes they had never returned to. Their initial raw feelings had evolved into a new perspective.

Since August 14, 1980, many families have had additional traumas—the death of a child or spouse, accidents, disease, addictions or acute family dysfunction. A few years after the flood, two mothers each lost a child in an accident. One said if she had known her child would be killed, she wished she would have died in the flood. The other mother admitted that it seemed unfair to survive the flood only to be forced to deal with the loss of her child.

Against all of life's trials, the flood acted as a benchmark for life's most horrific experiences.

SYMPTOMS OF TRAUMA

Symptoms of trauma were common among Brady's Bend residents. They were most frequently frightened by rain, especially heavy rain. Kelly McNaughton, a former sound sleeper, admitted that after the flood, she didn't sleep well for a long time. Even a light rain would make her shoot straight up in bed. It took years before she could sleep through the rain. Another said that hard rain brings thoughts of the flood. He's learned to live with this, even though it feels like a flashback. One man's driving habits changed. When driving through heavy rain and coming upon a depression in the roadway, he drives as fast as he can to get to the other side. For some time, he has worried about rising water until he arrives home. Another survivor avoids water as much as she can.

Brady's Bend's now–Gulf Coast resident Jim Martin admits that his Brady's Bend experience heightened his concern about floods. Now, he deals with hurricanes and tornadoes. When one of his homes was affected by a storm surge a few years ago, it brought back memories of Brady's Bend.

Homeowners along Sugar Creek continue to watch the rain, looking up or monitoring the banks of the creek for any signs of flooding, ready to run to higher ground. One woman described the unforgettable sensation of standing in the floodwaters with debris brushing against her legs.

Children suffered as much as adults. One kindergarten-age girl panicked at the sound of thunder or rain. This family's grown children still call their parents to inquire about their safety when it rains. A teenage boy got the skin disorder psoriasis immediately after the flood, and his mother is convinced it is from his trauma.

Dan and Paulette Lege's four-year-old daughter, who was devasted by the loss of her aunt, would panic when her parents were out of her sight, worried about the loss of them, too. The family sought counseling for her.

Many adults admitted to dreaming of the flood's horror. Two said that my 2024 interview caused them to have dreams about flood the night of our interview. One mother became so anxious after the flood that she became agoraphobic, irrationally afraid to leave her own home.

PUTTING WHAT'S IMPORTANT IN PERSPECTIVE

Among the trauma, individuals, families and the community remained resilient. The flood put what's important in life into perspective for many. Tina Custer admits that she was knocked back and humbled by the flood. She lost her car and her newly purchased dorm supplies. Yet her cousin Myrtle lost her parents and son, all washed away with the Custer home. Watching Myrtle's enduring approach to planning and attending her family's funerals and continuing with life left Tina in awe.

The catastrophe caused neighboring communities to put aside sports rivalries and individuals to look beyond past offenses so they could create a congregation of helpers. That congregation of helpers was unique, something that many hadn't experienced before or ever again.

Butch Robinson visited his friend Chris Henderson the day before the flood. Butch told Chris he had won a gun raffle and was having a hard time collecting his prize from the raffle organizers. Butch lamented that he'd probably not live long enough to get that gun. The next day, Butch was dead, putting the fragility of life on full display.

Young Barry Robinson, a father at eighteen, said that the loss of his uncle Butch made him aware that life can be short and that putting things that you enjoy off may result in never getting a chance to do them. It also made him realize the importance of supporting others.

Struck by how quick things can happen and how little time there is to plan any course of action, Kelly McNaughton said, "I always thought when people said flash flood, you had time to get out. You don't have time to get out. You have no time. You don't have time to react. That realization changes you, because you think things can happen so fast and you can lose things so quickly. You really do need to live for each day."

Rodney King cautioned against second-guessing yourselves or others' actions. When it comes to natural disasters, looking back in judgment on the choices that people make is fruitless. He said, "When something like the flood happens, especially at night, there's more reaction than thinking. Unless you've been in the same or another life and death situation, in making a split-second decision you do what you think is right at the time."

SCARS AND HOPELESSNESS

At the height of the floodwaters, emergency responders and those who watched others struggle to survive experienced feelings of hopelessness at their inability to reach those who needed them. The sound of regret remains in their voices today.

Small businessowners felt overwhelmed by the daunting task of rebuilding. Sadness and anger hung in the air. One son described the wind being taken out of his father's sails, never to return. "Looking back, if anybody had PTSD from that flood, it was my dad. When he walked to East Brady five days after the flood, I think that's when it occurred to him that we almost died." It took only minutes for the water to rise enough to sweep them away. His father walked around like someone who had lost all hope. After having so much passion for what he was doing, he lost interest in life. He was never the same. "He was crushed, but he never said anything, because people, especially men back then, really didn't talk about how they felt."

When Tina Custer drove her eighty-year-old grandfather, Earl, by where his brother Elrick Custer's house had sat, Earl never failed to point and say, "My brother lived there. He died in the flood." It took years for Earl to allow Tina to pull over and get out of the car.

For those who had lost family members, especially the children, Christmas and the holidays were never the same. A quietness and melancholy replaced celebration and joy.

AWE OF NATURE, INCREASED CAUTIOUSNESS

While some struggled, others became more cautious, with a new respect for nature. Residents who had seen the power of water and the damage caused by floods had firsthand knowledge that helped them cope with future floods, like 1985's West Virginia flood and 2017's Hurricane Harvey.

Seeing the impact of nature caused a sense of awe and respect. For some, it was the power and speed at which nature can change a life that changed them: Rodney King said, "I preach to my kids, you never challenge Mother Nature because you will lose." For others, it was seeing sediment covered peonies reemerge two years later as healthy and vibrant as ever that gave them hope.

Matt Switzer became more cautious and aware of his surroundings. He believes the suddenness Brady's Bend's flash flood left the biggest impact: "It made me more aware of my surroundings, no matter where I was." After he lost his sense of smell in 1984, he considered his heightened awareness a good thing. At his workplace, a piece of equipment caught fire behind him. Because he couldn't smell the smoke, his attention to the reactions of people around him was even more acute.

For some, while they didn't become afraid of the rain, their general demeanor became one of caution. After the flood, Monica Andreassi and Rodney King never second-guessed their intuition when it came to being careful, "If one of us thought we were going to do something, and then the other one said, 'Oh, I don't think we should do it,' we said, 'OK, we're not doing it.'" Their cautiousness pervaded for years.

For the Leges, their grandchildren wondered why they worried about people and safety. While both of their workplaces required safety awareness, the flood amplified their realization that bad things can and do happen.

Never Live in a Flood Plain

Forever wary of potential flooding, several survivors said that they refuse to live close to water. Although one loves being near a stream, they won't live by one. Another said the same: "I have never bought a home that was anywhere near a floodplain. No matter how small the stream. I'm gonna live on a hill."

Another man's respect for water or moving water was altered completely. He never considered himself a "river guy," even though he grew up near the Allegheny River. Now, he says, "If it's not a swimming pool, I probably don't get in." He's also more careful with water, particularly standing water, never driving through it. When he travels south and there is a hurricane warning, he leads the pack to leave, knowing firsthand that you can't protect yourself by staying in place.

A resident who had their eye on buying a piece of property changed their mind after they saw the effect of the flood on that property.

DEDICATION SERVICE
BRADYS BEND FLOOD MEMORIAL

SUNDAY AUGUST 18, 1985 2:00 pm

Invocation and Opening Remarks — Pastor Herb McClintick

Choral Interlude "CLEANSE ME" Presbyterian Choir

Scripture Lesson and Interpretation Psalm 46
Pastor David Smith

Prayer of Dedication Father Dan Mahoney

Choral Interlude "JUST A CLOSER WALK"
Presbyterian Choir

Benediction Pastor Richard Seigfried

DEDICATED THIS DAY IN THE MEMORY OF
MRS H LENORA CRISSMAN
MR AND MRS ELRICK CUSTER
CAROL ANN LEGE
JERRY POTTS, JR
MR AND MRS WILSON ROBINSON
AMY ROBINSON
BETTY KAUFMAN

We are pleased that you could all attend this service, and especially welcome our distinguished guests, PA Representative David Wright and PA Senator Tim Shaffer.

The Flood Memorial Committee invites you to a reception immediately following the service at the St Stephens Old Stone Church, where light refreshments will be served.

1985 Flood Memorial dedication. *Diane McClaine Miskiel.*

2024 Brady's Bend Flood Memorial. *Brady's Bend Township.*

AFTERWORD

After forty-four years, scars of Brady's Bend's 1980 flood are nearly invisible. Avalanched hillsides are now covered in greenery. Homes were restored long ago. A new purpose has transformed closed businesses, and the land made vacant by the loss of twelve homes. While three generations remember the flood, the survivors are declining in number. The youngest generations are rightly absorbed in their own busy lives. Yet this historic event that shaped a community deserves to be remembered and recorded.

After Elick and Birch Custer's deaths, their daughter Myrtle donated the Custer property to Brady's Bend Township for a memorial park dedicated to those who perished in the flood. In 1985, the park was completed with funds and labor donated by area businesses and families. A memorial stone was created and placed at the location. A beautiful commemoration ceremony and reception was held on August 18, 1985.

In 2019, a group of volunteers completed a fundraising effort and a park restoration, adding a pavilion, several park benches and grills for visitors looking for a quiet space to reflect, celebrate or relax.

Passing motorists zip by the memorial without a sideways glance, going about their business of the day. My hope is that there are family historians and storytellers among them who understand the value of sharing this past.

I also hope that other communities with similar experiences find some solace in knowing that their experiences are understood and shared by many others.

NOTES

Introduction

1. West Virginia Public Broadcasting, "Inside Appalachia: WV's 1,000 Year Flood," https://www.youtube.com/watch?v=V8ehFEtJsGo.

Chapter 1

2. James A. Smith, Mary Lynn Baeck, Alexandros A. Ntelekos, Gabriele Villarini and Matthias Steiner, "Extreme Rainfall and Flooding from Orographic Thunderstorms in the Central Appalachians," *Water Resources Research* 47, November 2010, 1.
3. "2 Dead in Connecticut After Flash Floods from 'Training Thunderstorms,'" *Pittsburgh Post-Gazette*, August 20, 2024, A8.
4. Bruce Schreiner and Timothy Easley, "Entire Communities Wiped Out by Massive Appalachian Floods, KARE11," Associated Press, July 29, 2022, https://www.kare11.com/article/news/nation-world/appalachian-floods/507-5cc50ced-d238-465c-a73d-99e8986b3d1c.
5. West Virginia Public Broadcasting, "Inside Appalachia."
6. *If These Hills Could Talk: A History of Brady's Bend Township, Perry Township and East Brady, Pennsylvania* (Brady's Bend Historical Society, 1984), 51.
7. *If These Hills Could Talk*, 67.

8. James M. Swank, "The Manufacture of Iron and Steel Rails in Western Pennsylvania," *The Pennsylvania Magazine of History and Biography* 28, no. 1 (1904): 4–5.
9. *If These Hills Could Talk*, 54.
10. *If These Hills Could Talk*, 42–48.
11. *If These Hills Could Talk*, 45.
12. "Brady's Bend Township, Armstrong County, Pennsylvania," United States Census Bureau, https://data.census.gov/profile/Brady's_Bend_township,_Armstrong_County,_Pennsylvania?g=060XX00US4200508152.
13. "How's My Waterway," United States Environmental Protection Agency, https://mywaterway.epa.gov/community/Brady's%20Bend,%20PA/overview.
14. "Peaceful Sugar Creek Becomes a Monster," *The Derrick*, August 16, 1980, 2.
15. "Western Pennsylvania," Wikipedia, https://en.wikipedia.org/wiki/Western_Pennsylvania.
16. Smith, Baeck, Ntelekos, Villarini and Steiner, "Extreme Rainfall and Flooding," 4.
17. Smith, Baeck, Ntelekos, Villarini and Steiner, "Extreme Rainfall and Flooding," 17.
18. John S. Pomeroy, "Storm-Induced Slope Movements at East Brady, Northwestern Pennsylvania," *U.S. Geological Survey Bulletin* 1,618 (1984): 1–3.
19. Pomeroy, "Storm-Induced Slope Movements," 3.
20. "To Summer: Glad to See Your Fall," *Pittsburgh Press*, September 21, 1980, 1.
21. "East Brady, Pennsylvania," Western Regional Climate Center, DRI Foundation, https://wrcc.dri.edu/cgi-bin/cliMAIN.pl?pa2363.
22. "Pittsburgh Weather in 1980," Extreme Weather Watch, https://www.extremeweatherwatch.com/cities/pittsburgh/year-1980#june.
23. "NOAA Atlas 14 Point Precipitation Frequency Estimates: KS," NOAA, https://hdsc.nws.noaa.gov/pfds/pfds_map_cont.html.
24. "Peaceful Sugar Creek Becomes a Monster," *The Derrick*, August 16, 1980, 2.
25. "Flash Flood Leaves Destruction," *Clarion News*, August 19, 1980, 11.
26. Forbes Tompkins and Brian Watts, "Flooding Is Nearly a Daily Occurrence Throughout the U.S.: New Analysis Shows That Flood Events Affect Communities Nationwide and Year-Round," Pew Trusts, https://www.pewtrusts.org/en/research-and-analysis/

articles/2022/12/15/flooding-is-nearly-a-daily-occurrence-throughout-the-us.

27. Charlotte Hall, "Geo Explainer: Are Hurricanes Getting Worse?" *Geographical*, September 7, 2023, https://geographical.co.uk/science-environment/geo-explainer-are-hurricanes-getting-worse; Tompkins and Watts, "Flooding Is Nearly a Daily Occurrence."
28. Pomeroy, "Storm-Induced Slope Movements," 1.

Chapter 2

29. "Flood Notice Was Delayed by Bad Luck," *Valley News Dispatch*, August 20, 1980, 1.
30. "Flood Victims in Brady's Bend Tell How Water Swept Through," *Butler Eagle*, August 16, 1980, 1.
31. "Area Declared Disaster Scene; Two Still Missing," *Butler Eagle*, August 16, 1980, 2.
32. "Flood Clean-Up Continuing, Updated Information Given," *Leader Vindicator*, September 3, 1980, 1.
33. "Woman Watched in Horror as Friends Died in Flooding," *The Derrick*, August 18, 1980, 1.
34. "Owner of Pezzuti's Store Says It's a Miracle She's Still Alive," *Butler Eagle*, August 13, 1981, 23.
35. "Flood Death Toll Climbs to Seven," *Valley News Dispatch*, August 16, 1980, A1.
36. "Flood Victims," *Butler Eagle*, 1; "Stimacs Lose Van, More," *Butler Eagle*, August 16, 1980, 1–2.
37. "Mudslide Move Buildings as Torrential Rains Fall," *Butler Eagle*, August 15, 1980, 1.
38. "Woman Watched in Horror," *The Derrick*, 1.
39. "Davis Alexander Palmer: Rescuer of Trapped Women Earned Carnegie Medal," *Butler Eagle*, August 13, 1981, 22.
40. Carnegie Hero Fund Commission, https://www.carnegiehero.org.
41. "Ken-L Ration," Wikipedia, https://en.wikipedia.org/wiki/Ken-L_Ration.
42. "In Brady's Bend, A Night of Raw Terror," *Post Gazette*, August 19, 1980, A1.

Chapter 3

43. "Brady's Bend Suffers Death and Destruction," *The Catholic Accent* 20, no. 11 (August 21, 1980): 1.
44. "Thornburg Pledges Cleanup Help," *Leader Times*, August 21, 2980.

Chapter 4

45. "Problems in Flood-Stricken Area Persist, Red Cross Workers Report," *Butler Eagle*, September 10, 1980, 21.
46. "Brady's Bend, Petroleum Valley Still Cleaning Up Debris," *Butler Eagle*, August 8, 1980, 1.
47. "Brady's Bend, Petroleum Valley Still Cleaning Up," Butler Eagle, 1.
48. "Federal Funds Available for Flood Victims," *Butler Eagle*, August 20, 1980, 1.
49. "Brady Water Restored as Cleanup Continues," *Leader Times*, August 25, 1980, 1.
50. "National Flood Insurance Program," Wikipedia, https://en.wikipedia.org/wiki/National_Flood_Insurance_Program.
51. "Flood Insurance Study: Township of Brady's Bend Pennsylvania, Armstrong County," Federal Emergency Management Agency, July 3, 1986, community number 421302.
52. Bob Henson, "Why Is It So Hard to Fix the National Flood Insurance Program?" Weather Underground, November 9, 2017, https://www.wunderground.com/cat6/why-it-so-hard-fix-national-flood-insurance-program.
53. Thomas Frank, "Hundreds of Thousands Drop Flood Insurance as Rates Rise," E&E News, August 17, 2022, https://www.eenews.net/articles/hundreds-of-thousands-drop-flood-insurance-as-rates-rise/.
54. "Town and Country," *Butler Eagle*, August 29, 1980, 8.
55. "New Sewage Plant Ready, Water System Complete," *Butler Eagle*, August 13, 1981, 22.

ABOUT THE AUTHOR

Since retiring after working for more than thirty years as a successful small business owner, Lisa Olszak Zumstein has found that her passion for local history and writing has been given time to bloom. Growing up with eight siblings in the tightly knit rural Appalachian community of Brady's Bend, Pennsylvania, Lisa has had hard work and resilience ingrained into everything she does. Drawing on her career as an interviewer, researcher, analyst and compelling writer, Lisa uncovers the broader significance of a 1980 catastrophic storm and flood in her hometown of Brady's Bend. With a talent for turning complicated technical information into clear, relatable terms, Lisa captures the emotional and long-term effects of catastrophic events on everyday life.